Godfrey Richard Park

The Church Bells of Holderness

Godfrey Richard Park

The Church Bells of Holderness

ISBN/EAN: 9783337403201

Printed in Europe, USA, Canada, Australia, Japan

Cover: Foto ©Lupo / pixelio.de

More available books at **www.hansebooks.com**

Annales Seigniorii Holdernessiæ.

THE CHURCH BELLS
OF
HOLDERNESS.

BY

GODFREY RICHARD PARK, Gent.

"I am but a gatherer and a disposer of
other men's stuff."—*Wotton.*

LONDON:
WILLIAM ANDREWS & CO., 5, FARRINGDON AVENUE, E.C.

1898.

TO

THE VENERABLE JAMES PALMES, D.D.,

ARCHDEACON

OF THE EAST RIDING OF YORKSHIRE,

THIS VOLUME

IS BY PERMISSION

RESPECTFULLY DEDICATED.

Preface.

THE bell is not the least interesting feature of the parish church. Yet, as a rule, it receives but slight notice from the architect, and unless it bears evidence of great antiquity or some marked peculiarity, but little attention from the antiquary or the archæologist.

During the past half century, one of the victims of the ardour for church restoration has not unfrequently been the old church bell. In some instances, ruthlessly disregarding the holy uses to which it had been devoted, the custodians have sold or disposed of it for secular purposes; and in others, carelessly ignoring the bell as a consecrated appurtenance to the church, they (the custodians) have caused it to be recast, and the sacred legend inscribed by their pious forefathers to be obliterated, and in its place to have substituted the name and address of the bell-founder as a matter of business advertisement, thus not only destroying a venerable object of interest to Churchmen, but also removing an ancient land-mark, so to speak, in the history of the church and parish.

In the following pages the author has attempted to give a brief account of the bells formerly used in the various services of the Church, including those which have been since the Reformation dispensed with in Protestant churches, as well as those used at the periodical ecclesiastical seasons and in commemoration of national events. To accomplish this, he is greatly indebted to the already published treatises on the subject, particularly "The Ecclesiastical Bell," by the Rev. Alfred Gally, D.D., and "English Church Furniture," by Edward Peacock, Esq., F.S.A. Extracts from these sources, it will be observed, have been in several instances made.

In the compilation of the inscriptions on the bells, the author has availed himself of the list of "Inscriptions on the Bells of the East Riding of Yorkshire," collected some twenty years ago by the Rev. W. C. Boulter, F.S.A., and published in the *Yorkshire Archæological Journal*. To Mr. Boulter he takes this opportunity of tendering his grateful thanks for having kindly given permission to make use of

PREFACE. iii

his collection, and also of acknowledging the courtesy of the editor of the above journal in sanctioning the publication of the same. The author trusts that the preservation of the inscriptions on the several church bells in the Rural Deaneries of Holderness will be interesting to the clergy, and also to that portion of the laity who have a reverential regard for those venerable relics of mediæval times.

With respect to the dedication of the several churches, the author has adopted the ascriptions given by the late Rev. Canon Raine in an article written by him on the " Dedication of Yorkshire Churches," in the *Archæological and Topographical Journal* (vol. II., page 180).

The author begs also to tender his best thanks to those clergymen and laymen who have most courteously rendered him valuable assistance. Amongst the former he would particularly refer to the Rural Deans of the Deaneries of Hedon and Hornsea, the Rectors of Winestead and Catwick, the Vicars of Aldborough, Mapleton, Marfleet, and Swine, and the Rev. D. J. Smith, of the Presbytery, Hedon; and amongst the latter Mr. F. A.

Scott, of Sutton; Mr. James Young, Withernsea; and Mr. Robinson Readhead, Flamborough.

And though last, by no means least, he begs to acknowledge with thanks the permission kindly accorded to him by the Archbishop to insert the "Office of the Dedication of a Peal of Bells as ordered by His Grace in the Diocese of York."

G. R. P.

Hedon,
December, 1897.

CHURCH BELLS.

CHAPTER I.

"Funera plango, Fulgura frango
Sabbata pango,
Excito lentos, Dissipo ventos
Paco cruentos."

"OF all the articles of furniture," says Dr. Gatty,[1] "connected with those venerable edifices in which men congregate for the purpose of Divine worship, no one is more worthy of notice or is more susceptible of illustrative description than the bell."

The church bell hangs for centuries in the grey and ivied tower, and expresses with its iron tongue, to successive generations by hourly strokes, the gradual flight of inexorable time. It calls men to the public services of the

[1] Paper read by the Rev. Alfred Gatty, D.D., at a meeting of the Yorkshire Architectural Society at Pontefract, August, 1855.

church, it rings a merry peal at their marriages, and tolls a solemn knell at their funerals, it rouses the son of labour to the fields at day-break, it invites him to his dinner at noon, and regularly announces to him the hour of his repose. Even those who neglect its holier summonses depend upon the church bell for their guidance in the every-day duties of life, and the same voice which thus reminds them of their various engagements, and is associated with all their experiences of enjoyment or of woe issued from the loop-holes of the church belfry, in the same tones of sympathy when it addressed their distant forefathers who now lie buried in the old churchyard.

The history of bells is one of the most interesting in the record of inventions, they were first heard of about the year 400.[1] Bells and their substitutes have been, and are used among all nations from the time of the earliest records, mingled with customs connected with war, religion, and domestic life, as may be

[1] Antiquary, vol. ii., p. 220.

CHURCH BELLS.

gathered from the rites, ceremonies, and customs of barbaric hordes.[1]

Legendary lore and tradition, as a matter of course, attach to almost every institution which refers to ancient times; thus, tradition attributes the invention of bells to Noah, to whom a command was given to strike on a bell with a piece of wood three times a day to summon his workmen to their labour in building their sacred Ark.[2]

Passing by this tradition, the first-known instance of the bell being applied to ecclesiastical purposes is in the services of the Tabernacle in the wilderness. Small golden bells were ordered to be attached to the robe of the high priest, to intimate to the congregation when he went "in unto the holy place before the Lord, and when he came out."[3]

The inscription 'Tuba Dei,' not unfrequently met with, refers to the well-known analogy between the bells of the Christian Church and the silver trumpets of the Levites. As the

---

[1] Antiquary, vol. ii., p. 18.   [2] *Vide* Fletcher's work on Ninivch.
[3] Exodus xxviii., 34-35.

silver trumpets gave the signal for holy convocations, and encouraged Israel of old to seek the promised land, so do our bells call us to church, and cheer us on our way to the heavenly Canaan.[1]

It may be observed that bells were never used in the ancient Jewish Church as a means of convoking the people to public worship, but trumpets of silver were ordained for that purpose.[2]

Nearly all writers on symbolism agree in considering that bells not only represent the Levitical trumpets in their sacred uses, but also in their analogy to the living messengers of God, who have to lift up their voice as a trumpet.[3]

Although bells were doubtless in common use among the heathen, they played only a rare or subordinate part in their religious services, and it was not until the Roman Empire became Christian, and the storm of persecution ceased, that the faithful Christians,

---

[1] Yorks. Arch. and Topo. Jour., 11, 6.   [2] Numbers x., 2.
[3] Isaiah lviii., 1.

who, during the time of danger, had hidden themselves in woods and deserts, and secret caves, appeared in public, rebuilt the churches which had been levelled with the ground, founded, erected, and finished the temples of the holy martyrs, and, as it were, displayed their conquering ensigns in all places; they celebrated festivals and performed their sacred rites "with clean hearts and mouths";[1] then it may reasonably be inferred that hearers would be summoned by the sonorous bidding of the bell.

During the fifth century, St. Patrick, the Apostle of Ireland, distributed church bells in that country.[2] The Abbot Cumian, in his life of Columba, written about the year 657, alludes in such a manner to the use of bells for assembling the brotherhood to religious worship, as would lead directly to the inference that belfries must have existed in St. Columba's time.[3]

---

[1] Bede's Ecclesiastical Hist., edited by Dr. Giles.
[2] Petries round towers of Ireland, pp. 32, 339.
[3] Columba was an Irish priest and monk of the sixth century, he built a church and monastery at Iona, of which he became the Abbot; he died in 597.

Du Cange says that it is uncertain who introduced bells, but they were invented by the Italians, the large ones in Campania, and the small ones in Nola; others say that they came into use in the seventh century, and that Bede is our first author who mentions them.[1]

In England there appears no earlier notice of church bells than that of Bede. The venerable historian alludes to the well-known sound of the bell by which they were accustomed to be summoned to prayers.[2]

St. Dunstan in the tenth century is said to have given bells to many churches, and to have furnished Malmesbury Abbey with a peal of bells of his own casting. He directed in his rule for the reformation of monasteries that at mass, nocturns, and vespers, from the feast of the Innocents to the Circumcision, all bells should be rung as was the custom in England.

Early bell founding, like other scientific crafts, was carried on by the monks. St. Dunstan was a skilful artificer. When in after times

---

[1] Bingham's Antiquities, 1, 316.
[2] Ven. Bede's Eccl. Hist. of Britain.

bell founding became a regular trade, some founders were itinerant, travelling from place to place where they found business, but the majority had settled works in large towns.[1]

During the Middle Ages bells became objects of veneration, and were not only blessed and exorcised, but names were assigned to them through the medium of the baptismal rite, and anointing with holy oil, often performed by the highest dignitaries of the Church. The blessing or baptism of bells is an ancient and interesting ceremony, the bells about to be blessed were placed in a convenient position in the church; the miserere and other psalms were recited or sung, after which the bishop washed the bells within and without with a linen cloth, previously dipped in holy water, the choir in the meantime singing the 145th and 146th psalms. The bells were then anointed with holy oil, the choir chanting the Antiphon 'Vox Domino super aquas multas,' together with the 28th psalm, after which the bells were again anointed in the form of a cross seven times. Incense was then

[1] Chambers's Book of Days, 1, 301.

put in the thurible and placed under the bells, which ended the ceremony.[1] After these ceremonies, it was believed that the evil spirits lurking in the air might be driven away by their sound.[2]

At the baptism of a bell, certain prayers were used for blessings on it. Part of one of these curious prayers put up for the bell at its baptism is mentioned in Hone's every-day book :—[3]

"Lord grant that wheresoever this holy bell thus washed (or baptised) and blessed shall sound, all deceits of Satan, all danger of whirlwind, thunders, lightnings, and tempests may be driven away, and that devotion may increase in Christian men when they hear it, etc., etc. . . . O Lord, pour upon it thy heavenly blessing that the fiery darts of the Devil may be made to fly backwards at the sound thereof. And that it may deliver from danger of wind and thunder, etc. . . . And grant Lord that all who come to the church at the sound of it may

[1] Arch. Jour., iv., 49. [2] History of Crowland Abbey.
[3] vol. ii., 141.

be free from all temptations of the Devil, etc."

The Roman custom of consecrating bells is not earlier than the tenth century, and the names of men and women were given to them.[1] A bell in St. Mark's Church, Lincoln, is always spoken of as "Old Kate." "Great Tom of Lincoln," a bell in the Cathedral of that city, is one of the most celebrated in England.[2]

At Meaux Abbey, under William, the ninth Abbot, 1249-1269, the bell tower covered with lead, was added to the church, and within it was placed a great bell called 'Benedictus.' And William of Scarborough, the eighteenth Abbot of Meaux, 1372-1396, caused a great bell named 'Jesus' to be cast; his successor, Thomas Burton, 1396-1399, cast from the bell metal that had been left by his predecessor (William of Scarborough) three new bells to accord with the big bell 'Jesus.' They were termed, 1, 'Mary,' weighing 1,500 lbs. ; 2, 'John,' weighing 1,200 lbs. ; and 3, 'Benedictus,' weighing

---

[1] Frosbroke's Encyclopedia of Antiquities, 1, 230.
[2] Reliquary, vol. vii., p. 138.

900 lbs., expending over their manufacture £16 17s. 6d.[1]

The consecration of bells is now very properly revived and substituted for baptism. The ceremony of consecration was performed at Burton Pidsea in Holderness by the Bishop of Hull (Dr. Blunt) in 1891, when the recastings of the old bells were placed in the church there.

In the mediæval ages, there was a certain amount of superstition attached to church bells, they were supposed to possess an exorcising power, and would cause fiends to decamp. To this superstition the origin of the passing bell, anciently rung on the Christian's mortal agony, may reasonably be traced, the ringing of the bell being regarded as able to scare away evil spirits, who might otherwise disturb the departing soul.

Bells had also assigned to them a protective, or even an intercessory character. They were supposed to ward off or allay thunder storms, and were wont to be rung in the Middle Ages

---

[1] Dr. Cox in transactions of the East Riding Antiquarian Society, vol. i., pp. 32, 57.

to drive away thunder. Among the German peasantry the sign of the cross is used to dispel a thunder storm. Several bells in Lincolnshire and some in Yorkshire are marked with the fylfot or cross of Thor; it is of a singular shape in imitation of the hammer of Thor the thunderer.[1] None so far have been found to possess this mark in Holderness. The following entry appears in the accounts of the churchwardens of Spalding, Lincolnshire, in 1519:—

"Itm p^d for ryngyng when the tempest was iij^d."

"If that thunder chanc'd to rore and stormie tempest shake,
A wonder is it for to see the wretches how they quake,
Howe that no fayth at all they have nor trust in aney thing,
The Clarke doth all the belles forthwith at once in steeple ring
With wond'rous sound and deeper farre than he was wont before,
Till in the loftie heavens darke, the thunder brays no more,

---

[1] Baring Gould's curious myths of the Middle Ages. Legend of the Cross, p. 89.

> For on those christen'd belles, they think doth lie such power and might,
> As able is the tempest great and storme be vanquish'd quight."[1]

Bells also bore a prominent part in the censures administered by the Church. Excommunication by "bell, book, and candle" being the heaviest malediction. When a priest declared any person excommunicated, the people were summoned together by the sound of a "bell;" the excommunication was pronounced from a "book;" and all "candles" were extinguished by throwing them on the ground, with an imprecation that the person on whom excommunication was about to be pronounced might be extinguished or destroyed by the wrath of God.[2]

There was also the old custom of swearing by the bell. Chaucer alludes to this custom; he makes the famous host of the "Tabard" thus speak:—

> "Ye quod our hoste by Seint Poules belle
> Ye say right soth."[3]

---

[1] Hone, E.D.B., II, 136. [2] Penny Post, vol. xvi., p. 307.
[3] Canterbury Tales.

It is quite clear from the " Inventarium Monumentorum Superstitionis," alluded to in Mr. Peacock's exhaustive treatise on church furniture,[1] that at the time of the Reformation many church bells were destroyed, but perhaps as great sacrilege in our churches was committed during the Civil War, when many church bells were molten down and cast into cannon, by fanatical Puritans who, judging from their ruthless removal of ornaments, and by their purloining of brass memorials from churches, appear to have been influenced by motives of plunder rather than by a spirit of patriotism or piety.

Every person who has any reverence for sacred things cannot but deplore the wanton destruction and profane desecration of the furniture of the church by religious zealots at the two exciting periods in the history of our country, the Reformation and the Civil War. If the fierceness of religious hate had spared the ornaments of the Church, they would now have been valued. Thus one

[1] English Church Furniture, by Edward Peacock, F.S.A.

generation, in the fury of its blind zeal, sweeps away what its successors would treasure with reverence and love.'

The sacrilegious spirit of the people will in a great measure account for the fact that the greater number of church bells in Holderness bear dates subsequent to these exciting times. A few pre-Reformation bells are, however, still to be found in the Seigniory, *e.g.*, Easington Elsternwick, Halsham, and Sproatley, in the rural deanery of Hedon; and Catwick, and Leven in the rural deanery of Hornsea; which, although they bear no date, may be reasonably inferred from the inscriptions and the character of the letters on them to have existed previous to the Reformation. There are, however, a few bells which bear the names of saints evidently of a date after the Reformation, *e.g.*, Atwick, Aldborough, Riston, and Winestead, but the greater number appear to have been placed in the several churches during the latter half of the seventeenth century.

It is scarcely probable that any bells now

1 Fasciculi Zizaniorum, xiv., xxxviii. Peacock, 83n.

remain in this country of a date prior to the fourteenth, or at most the thirteenth, century. The custom of inserting the date in the inscription was not observed until late in the sixteenth century. The inscriptions on the oldest bells are in Lombardic and black letter character, the former probably the more ancient. The black letter was superseded by the ordinary Roman capitals towards the close of the sixteenth century. After the Reformation, the inscriptions are rendered in English; the founders then frequently placed their own names on the bells, often with some rhyme or sentiment.

There were, in the mediæval ages, numerous bells attached to the various services of the Church, *e.g.*, the Marriage bell, the Passing bell, the Priest's bell, the Litany bell, the Sermon bell, the Saunce bell, the Sanctus bell, the Agnus bell, the Sacring bell, the Jesus bell, the Howslinge bell, and the Ave bell. Of these, only the Marriage and the Passing bell are as a rule used in Protestant churches.

The periodical ecclesiastical seasons were

formerly, and in some cases still are, observed by the ringing of the church bells, *e.g.*, Christmas Day, All Hallows Eve (now as a rule discontinued), and Good Friday.

The commemoration of state events, the Queen's birthday, accession, and coronation, is still celebrated by peals of church bells. The anniversaries of the restoration of the Royal family on 29th of May (Royal Oak Day), the escape of King James I. from the Gowrie Plot on 5th of August, and the Gunpowder Plot on 5th of November are now, as a rule, discontinued.

The observance of state services was considered in the Lower House of Convocation in 1857, and the report of a committee was presented on the 10th of July in that year, which stated that the observance of these services rested on the authority of the Crown. The subject was debated in Parliament in June, 1859, which resulted in an address to the Crown from both Houses, praying for their discontinuance. A Royal warrant, authorising such discontinuance, was issued on 17th of

January, 1859. In consequence of this warrant, the enactments requiring the observance of these days were, in 1859, repealed.[1]

Local events also come in for their share of joyous peals of bells, such as Episcopal visitations, Mayor-choosings, and sometimes even Parliamentary elections, and the like.

To these various bells may be added the Easter or Vestry bell on Easter Monday. The Curfew bell every evening, the Pancake bell on Shrove Tuesday, the Harvest bell in the harvest season, and the ringing of the church bell by the new Incumbent on his induction to the church and living.

The chief use to which church bells are now devoted in our parish churches is the calling together of the parishioners for the purpose of divine worship, and in connection with the various services of the church, especially those of marriage and the burial of the dead. " Laudo verum. Plebem voco. Congrego clerum. Defunctos ploro pestem fugo. Festa decoro," *i.e.*, I praise the true God. I call the people.

[1] 22 Vict. Cap., 2.

I congregate the clergy. I bemoan the dead. I enliven the festivals.[1]

The cheerful Sabbath bells, wherever heard, strike pleasant on the sense, most like the voice of one who, from the far-off hills, proclaims tidings of good to Sion.[2]

And here it may be remarked that on the occasion of calling the congregation together on Sundays and Holy days, the bells should be chimed, there should be no ringing on such occasions. An old rhyme well expresses the lawful and proper use of bells.[3]

> "To call the folks to church in time
> We chime.
> When mirth and joy are on the wing
> We ring.
> When from the body parts the soul
> We toll."

In some remote places where the rude little church would have no belfry accommodation, or where the sparse population dwelt widely apart, the people were summoned to divine service by the perambulating bell-man. The

---

[1] Strutt's Sports and Pastimes, p. 292.
[2] Charles Lamb.
[3] Said to be inscribed on a bell in Durham Cathedral.

ringer went about on a Sunday with a hand-bell, which he rung as he walked, and proclaimed his holy errand. A bell of this description still exists at Flamborough in the East Riding, which was used for this purpose until about the year 1845.[1]

The Marriage Bell.

A peal of bells on the celebration of a wedding, being a time of mirth and joy, is an ancient custom, and is still in full force. Allusion to the marriage ceremony is to be found sometimes on church bells, *e.g.*, at Hedon, the legend on the 2nd bell probably refers to marriage as well as to funerals, "wind (*i.e.*, win) them and bring them, and I will ring for them."

The Passing Bell.

In pre-Reformation times, the Passing bell, instead of being rung as now, after death, was sounded when a person was supposed to be at the point of death, in order that the people hearing it might be enabled to pray for a soul so soon to be beyond human aid, and where

[1] Ex. information of Mr. Readhead of Flamborough.

naught but prayer might avail it anything. After the spirit had returned to Him who gave it, the 'Soul bell' was tolled, so that again, when all was over, the living might pray for the repose of the dead. The following quotation illustrates this custom :—

> "Pray for the soul of Sir John le Spring,
> When the black monks sing, and the chantry bells ring.
> Pray for the sprite of the murdered knight,
> Pray for the rest of Sir John le Spring.
>
> And aye the Mass Priest sings his song,
> And patters many a Prayer,
> And the chantry bell tolls loud and long,
> And aye the lamp burns there."[1]

The Passing bell is tolled at Hedon either immediately after death, or the evening before the funeral, on the first or sixth bell, according to the rank of the deceased. The following curious order was made at Hedon in 1687, relative to the tolling of the bells in case of death :—

"At this Sessions, it is ordered by us, whose names are hereunder written, that when any person shall happen to dye, for which there

[1] Surtees.

shall be any of the bells rung, the relation of the deceased, or any person concerned, shall pay to the churchwardens, for the tyme beinge, for and towards maintayninge of the bells belonging to St. Augustine's Church in Hedon aforesaide, as hereinafter set downe and expressed; that is to say, for the first bell, (now commonly called the 'poor bell,') sixpence; the seconde bell, one shilling; the thyrde bell, two shillings; the fowerth bell, three shillings; the fyfth bell, fower shillings; and the sixth, or greate bell, fyve shillings. Robert Ombler, Maior; John Medley, Minister; Benia Gibson, Martin, x Robinson, Churchwardens."[1]

The fee for the bell appears to be a very ancient custom at Hedon, for in the account of the keepers of the fabric of St. Augustine, temp., 32 Henry VI., is found the following item:—

"And ij^s received for tolling the greate bell, viz., for the obits of Robert Baty, Katharine Bolton, Robert Cromwell, and others this year."[2]

A smaller fee is still paid for the tolling of the poor bell to the sexton, but not to the church-

[1] Park's Hist. of Hedon, 297.   [2] ib, 298.

wardens. A similar custom was (if not now) observed at St. Mary's Church, Hull, as appears from the following extracts from the registers there :—

"1642. Nov. 17th, John Jackson, Surgeon, with grete bell buried."

"1643. Nov. 7th, Metres Chambers with great bell buried."

"Feb. 12th, Rebecca, ye d. of Sir Mathew Boynton, in the Quier with great bell."[1]

It is the custom in many places, on the tolling of the Passing bell, to indicate, by strokes on the bell after the knell, the sex of the deceased, and thus the knell is said to be 'told,' or counted; the custom in many places, as at Hedon, is to strike on the bell three strokes for a child of either sex, six for a woman, and nine for a man, hence, no doubt, arises the common saying that "nine tailors make a man," which is really an inaccurate way of saying "nine tellers make a man," alluding to the nine strokes on the bell when a man's knell is rung. With reference

[1] Register of St. Mary's, Hull, Arch. Jour., vol. xii., p. 468.

to the tolling twice for a man, and thrice for a woman, an old English homily for Trinity Sunday, quoted by Strutt, has the following :—

"Ye fourme of ye Trinitie was founden in manne, that was Adam, our forefadir of erth, oon personne and Eve of Adam ye seconde personne, and of them both was the third personne. At ye death of a manne three bellis should be rong at his knell in worsehippe of ye Trinitie and for a woman who was ye second persone of ye Trinitie two bellis should be rungen."

The legend on the second bell in Hedon Church "wind them (i.e. wrap them in the winding sheet) and bring them and I will ring (i.e. toll) for them," evidently alludes to the Passing bell as well as probably to the Marriage bell. A short peal of muffled bells is sometimes rung immediately after the burial. Of muffling bells there is no precedent in antiquity. Brand thinks it was introduced after the Restoration.[1]

[1] Fosbroke, I, 230.

THE PRIEST'S BELL

was a bell formerly rung for a few minutes immediately after the bells had ceased chiming for service, to intimate that the priest was about to commence the service. The custom is still continued at Hedon, although it has often been erroneously called the "Mayor's bell," According to local tradition the Mayor left his residence on the ringing of this bell which continued to be rung until his worship entered the sacred edifice.

THE LITANY BELL

was in ancient times rung after morning prayers. In later times it was a custom in several churches to toll a bell whilst the Litany was being read to give notice to the people that the Communion service was coming on.[1]

THE SERMON BELL

was a small bell hung in the belfry, which was wont to be rung after the Nicene creed, to call in the Dissenters to hear the sermon. In the last century, Nonconformists besides frequenting

---

1 Southey.

the meeting house often times attended the sermon at church.

THE SAUNCE BELL.

The Priest when he sped him to say his service rang the "Saunce bell," and spake out aloud "Pater Noster," by which token the people were commanded silence, reverence, and devotion. According to Staveley and Warton this bell was rung when the Priest came to "Holy, Holy, Holy, Lord God of Sabaoth," in order that persons might know that the "Canon" (or consecration prayer) was commencing, they then bowed the head and spread or elevated their hands and said, "Salve lux mundi, etc." "Hail light of the world, etc."[1]

THE SANCTUS BELL

was rung to warn the people of the elevation of the host at the parish Mass. It was fixed outside the church frequently on the apex of the eastern gable of the nave: bell cotes made to contain the Sanctus bell yet remain at Boston and Goxhill in Lincolnshire. This bell was

[1] Peacock's Church Furniture, 252.

rung at the words "Sanctus, Sanctus, Sanctus, Dominus Deus Sabaoth," to excite the attention of the people to acts about to take place as well as to notify the fact to the parishioners who were unable to attend the service.[1] The same bell has been sometimes named the "Agnus Bell," so called by reason of its being rung at the elevation. In the certificate of ornaments in the Church of Hemswell, Lincolnshire :

"Itm one Agnus bell gone owtt of the foresayd Churche, no man knoweth how. Ano Domi one thousand five hundrethe three schore and foure."[2]

THE SACRING BELL,

a hand bell rung at the elevation of the host, sometimes called the "Altar bell."

> "Her eyes were bright as the merry sunlight,
> When it shines on the dewy grass,
> And her voice was clear as the 'Sacring bell,'
> That is rung at the Holy Mass."[3]

The size of these hand bells may to a certain extent be gathered from the profane use made

---

[1] Ritual reason why, 263. [2] Peacock's Church Furniture, 103.
[3] Ibim, 252.

of them at the time of the Reformation, *e.g.* in the return of the churchwardens of the parish of Hemswell before mentioned of the monuments of superstition.

"Itm ij hande belles solld to Robert Astroppe one off the sayd churche wardens to make a mortar off and they be defaced the same yere by the condecent off the holle pes" (parish).

In a like return of the parish of Harborough.

"Itm Sacringe bell wch Thomas Carter had and he hath made a horse bell thereof to hang at a horse's eare."

And in a similar return for the parish of Hoge.

"Itm a Sacringe bell sold to Austin Earle to put about a calves neck."

In a like account of the parish of Waddingham in 1566.

"Itm one sacringe bell wch honge at a Maypole toppe and what has become thereof we know not."

In the Churchwardens account of S. Mary's, Stamford, A.D. 1428, "et Thos. harpmaker p. emendacie de le schafte, xjd."

The shaft or maypole was in former times part of the public property of the parish, and as such repaired by the churchwardens. Popular amusements were in those days under the patronage of the church and had in many cases a half-religious character. May games though much older than the Christian Church were connected with some of its most pleasing rites. Maypoles seem to have existed in most of our villages until the time of our great Civil War. By an ordinance of the Long Parliament, 6th April, 1644, all Maypoles were ordered to be removed as "heathenish vanities generally abused to superstition and wickednesse."[1]

THE JESUS BELL.

The Jesus bell is probably very much the same as the Sanctus bell; the origin is to be found in the order of Pope Urban II., A.D. 1095, re-enforced by Pope Gregory IX. in the time of the Crusades, as recorded by Matthew of Paris,

[1] Peacock's Church Furniture, 179.

in honour of the Incarnation of Jesus, hence, perhaps, the Jesus bell. The probability is, that in this province the Jesus bell was rung (and not the Sanctus bell) immediately before the Canon of consecration, and that in the northern district the Sanctus bell was not used until after the Berengarian controversy, which resulted in the two elevations, and therefore necessitated the use of another bell as another warning to inform the faithful of the completion of the consecration.[1] In the Cathedral of Richmond, there was a bell called the Jesus bell, placed there in the reign of King Edward VI. (this would be after the Reformation), the inscription upon it was:—

> "I am the bell of Jesus, and Edward is our King,
> Sir Thomas Heywood first caused me to ring."

In St. Paul's Cathedral, four great Jesus bells were suspended; it is said that King Henry VIII. staked these famous bells, 'Jesus campanile,' at St. Paul's, against the great 'Folkmote bell' at hazard, and lost them to Sir Miles Partridge, who pulled them down, and sold

[1] Rev. A. B. Prole.

them for a large profit. In another account it is said that the bells were staked against £100. In Catwick Church the inscription on the bell there is "Campana Jhesu Christi."

THE HOWSLINGE BELL.

In the inventory of the monuments of superstition in the church of Gonwarbie, there appears (inter alia) "One howslinge bell, one sacring bell, ij hand bells." This bell was rung before the Holy Eucharist, when taken to the sick. At Manton, in a similar schedule, the following entry appears :—" Itm, a hames hudde and Tickynge belle, solld to Wyll^{m.} brombye and Edward poste, Anno domi, a thousande, ffyve hundreth, thresschore and fowre, John Mautson and Wyll^{m.} brumbye the churchwardens, and they be defaced." The "Tickynge belle" was probably one of the small bells before alluded to. "Hames hudde," a learned correspondent suggests that this may signify the block of wood to which small bells were usually attached.[1] In the inventory before

[1] Peacock, 250.

CHURCH BELLS. 31

referred to, frequent mention is made of "Hand bells," they are met with in nearly every inventory, and generally two in each church. Small bells were used for sacred purposes by the Celtic missionaries, and are closely identified with Christianity in this country.[1] These bells were used principally in processions, and were rung by the clerk or sexton solemnly at the intervals of every psalm sung in funeral processions. Previous to the Reformation, a small bell called the "Lyche bell," or "Corse bell," was usually rung before the corpse on the way to burial.[2]

THE AVE BELL.

The Ave bell is said to have been tolled three times during the day, of which in a morning whosoever should say three times the whole salutation of our Lady, "Ave Marie gratia plena, etc.," at six o'clock, three Aves at twelve o'clock at noon, and at six in the evening as many, for every time so doing should have three hundred days of pardon.[3] This bell is probably

---

[1] Notes on an ancient Celtic bell, by R. Quicke, Jour. Brit. Arch. Soc., N.S., vol. ii., p. 34.
[2] Arch. Jour., 48, 52.   [3] Yorks. Weekly Post, 4, 5, 95.

the same as the "Angelus bell," traditionally rung three times a day, morning, noon, and night, for the faithful to recite the angelic salutation in thankful remembrance of the Incarnation.

> "Hark! the bell is ringing,
> While the lark is singing
>   At the break of day.
> Joyfully repeating
> The Archangel's greeting:
>   Let us kneel and pray.
>
> Hark! at noon-tide pealing,
> Through the night air stealing,
>   Servant of the Lord,
> Be thy sole endeavour
> To do His will for ever,
>   According to His word.
>
> Yet again it calleth
> When the daylight falleth,
>   Seeming now to say
> The Son of God was given
> To make thee heir of heaven:
>   Mortal, kneel and pray."[1]

Among the several occasions on which church bells were wont to be rung was the well-known Curfew bell, "that tolls the knell

[1] Penny Post, vol. xxix., pp. 193, 219.

of parting day," in former times rung every evening.

The Curfew Bell.

The ringing of which has long since fallen into disuse. A law was passed soon after the Conquest to couvre le feu, and on the ringing of the couvre le feu, or Curfew bell, at eight o'clock in the winter, and nine in the summer, every person was obliged to cover up his fire, and stir abroad no more. In later times, this bell was rung to invite the parishioners to say a " De profundis," or other prayer for the souls of the departed. At the ringing of the couvre le feu in the evening, and the tolling of the " Ave " in the morning, the people were directed to say the Lord's Prayer and the salutation of the virgin five times. This bell has been frequently confounded with the " Harvest bell," which is still rung in many parishes.

The Harvest Bell

is, in many parishes, rung during the harvest season, night and morning, usually at five o'clock in the morning, and at seven in the evening.

The bell was rung at five a.m. for the purpose of celebrating Mass at that early hour, to enable the labourer to go to his work at the usual hour of six; and the evening bell to remind him to attend evensong after the labours of the day. Our forefathers never allowed their bells to be used for exclusively secular purposes.[1] A bell is rung at Preston during the summer and autumn seasons with which an interesting legend is connected.[2] A bell at Friskney, in Lincolnshire, has the inscription, "Laborem signo et requiem."[3] In a terrier of North Frodingham in 1786: "The Clerk's accustomary wages paid by the parishioners are two wheat sheaves for every oxgang of corn in the town field for ringing the harvest bell."

The Pancake Bell,

rung on Shrove Tuesday, the day before the commencement of Lent. In some places it is the custom (a custom which up to a very recent period was observed at Hedon) for the

---

[1] Rev. Dr. Cox, F.S.A., East Riding Antiquarian Society's Transactions, vol. iii., p. 16.
[2] Vide Preston Post. [3] Reliquary 8, 22.

senior apprentice in the town to ring the Pancake bell at eleven o'clock in the forenoon. The origin of the ringing of this bell is somewhat obscure; some ascribe its origin to the offering of cakes by the Pagan Saxons to the sun. Fosbroke's opinion is that pancakes are taken from the Fornacalia, in memory of the practice in use before the Goddess Fornax invented ovens. Shrove Tuesday being the vigil of Ash Wednesday, and a day on which everyone was bound to confess and be shrove or shriven (hence Shrove Tuesday); that none might plead forgetfulness of this duty, the great bell was rung at an early hour in every parish church. And although at the Reformation the shriving was not enjoined, yet the bell still continued to be rung on Shrove Tuesday, to remind (as it is said) the good wives of the annual fast, and that it was time to prepare the pancakes, hence the connexion of the apprentice with the Pancake bell. In the year 1406, Simon Eyre, then being Lord Mayor of London, is said to have instituted the observance of Shrove Tuesday as the apprentices' holiday. He ordered that, on the ringing of a bell about noon, all apprentices should leave off work for the day.[1] Shrove Tuesday being the last day before the solemn season of Lent, a sort of carnival was held on that day, when a feast of pancakes would probably be a prominent factor preparatory to the impending forty days' fast, and hence the apprentices would avail themselves of the opportunity of ringing this bell by way of a reminder to their mistresses to prepare the pancake feast.[2] Shrove Tuesday was a great day for rural sports, amongst which the cruel and barbarous pastime of "throwing at cocks" was universally practised. There appears to have been a custom for the apprentices and young men of York to ring one of the cathedral bells, which they called the Pancake bell. Dr. Lake, Vicar of Leeds and Prebendary of York, afterwards Bishop of Chichester, whilst at York Minster, in order to preserve discipline and good order in the church, determined to abolish irreverent customs, where-

---

[1] Annals of Yorks., vol. ii, p. 104.
[2] Strutt's Sports and Pastimes, 284.

by he incurred the ill-will of the vulgar. Dr. Lake continued to reside in York until he succeeded in convincing his adversaries that they must not convert the house of God into a place of idle riot.[1] In Halifax there was a popular rhyme with reference to the inauguration of Shrove-tide festivities :

> "When pancake bell begins to ring
> All Halifax lads begin to sing."[2]

Of the ringing of bells at the periodical ecclesiastical seasons, none is more universally observed than the joyous season of Christmas, when a merry peal of bells from the belfry greets the ear in almost every parish in the country.

CHRISTMAS DAY.

It is the custom at Hedon to ring a peal of bells every evening during the week before Christmas, and to usher in the Christmas morning and the new year with a peal immediately after the clock strikes twelve at midnight. This custom has its origin in pre-Reformation times, when on Christmas Day all people were

---

[1] Taylor's Yorks Anecdotes, p. 228. The Bishop died 30th August, 1689.   [2] ib.

called up at midnight to nocturnes (or more properly, matins) at this hour by the ringing of the bells, a birthday congratulation to the King of kings. There is perhaps no sound of bells more solemn and touching than the peal which rings out the old and ushers in the new year. Dr. Drake observes that the ushering in of the new year with rejoicings, presents, and good wishes, was a custom observed in the sixteenth century, and was as cordially celebrated in the court of the prince, as in the cottage of the peasant.[1]

Good Friday.

On Good Friday the custom at Hedon is to ring a muffled peal immediately before morning prayers.

Easter Monday.

The parishioners in every parish are summoned on Easter Monday for the purpose of choosing churchwardens. A bell is also rung to announce the holding of vestry meetings.

Among the records of the Tower of London

[1] Shakespeare and his times.

there still exists a curious document dated 39 Henry III. (1255), whereby the King granted to the brethren of the Guild of Westminster, who were appointed to ring the great bell of Westminster, that they shall receive every year 100s. from the royal treasury, viz., 50s. at Easter and 50s. at Michaelmas.

All Hallows.

The church bells used to be rung all night long on the festival of All Hallows; the custom ceased it would seem before the Reformation.

The state occasions on which church bells are usually rung are principally "The Queen's Birthday," 24th May; "The Queen's Accession," 20th June; and "The Queen's Coronation," 28th June. These manifestations of loyalty are, however, gradually falling into disuse in many places.

Royal Oak Day,

29th May, the anniversary of the restoration of the royal family, was formerly kept in remembrance by the church bells being rung.

An entry in the accounts of the churchwardens of S. Mary at Stamford in 1709: "Pd. Richard Hambleton for ale for ye ringers on ye 29 May, 00. 06. 00."[1]

The Gowrie Plot.

In some parts of the country bells were rung on 5th August to celebrate the escape of King James I. from the Gowrie Plot.

The Gunpowder Plot.

The anniversary of the Gunpowder Plot, 5th November, was half a century ago celebrated by general bell ringing all over the country; to this day bonfires are lighted and Guy Fawkes is still burnt in effigy. At Hedon up to about thirty years ago the bells were rung on 17th November according to the old style, a large fair was held on that day. A bell at Owmby, in Lincolnshire, bearing the date of 1687, has on it an inscription: "Let us remember the 5th of November;" and an entry in the accounts of the churchwardens at Stamford in 1608: "Itm paid for ryngyng the 5th of November, vi^d."[2]

[1] Reliquary, 7, 137.   [2] Vide page 16 ante.

CHURCH BELLS.   41

Church bells are also rung in celebration of local events, such as "Episcopal visitations," "Mayor choosings," and the like, and in some instances (with questionable taste), on the occasion of "Parliamentary elections."

Previous to 1860, the bell ringers at Hedon were paid by the Corporation an annual salary of eight guineas, for which they were required to ring on the following days and occasions, viz.: Queen's Birthday; Queen's Accession; Queen's Coronation; 29th May; 5th November; Christmas Eve; and New Year's Eve from 5 to 8 p.m.; Christmas Morn and New Year's Morn; the Archdeacon's Visitation; and the Archbishop's Confirmation when held; on the Mayor Choosing Day from 8 to 10 a.m. and 4 to 6 p.m.; and on each of the Audit Days from 8 to 11 a.m.'

A new incumbent on being inducted to his church and benefice, signifies his having taken legal possession thereof by locking the church door and tolling the bell. The ringing of the bell on such occasions appears to be an ancient

---

1 Park's History of Hedon, p. 299.

custom: "And on the day after the feast of S. John, A.D. 1131, the monks chose an abbot from among themselves and brought him into the church in procession; they sung the Te Deum laudamus, rang the bells, and set him in the abbot's seat."[1]

The induction of the vicar to the living of Hedon in 1676 is thus recorded: "In corporalem, realem, actualem, plena^m et pacificam possessionem ecclesiæ de Hedon cum omnibus suis membris pertinentiis jurib^s et comodis quibuscunq decimo tertio die Decembris Ano Domini 1676 inductus fuit Thos. Swinburne A.M."

CHANGE RINGING.

The number of changes that can be rung on bells is perhaps surprising to the uninitiated. On three bells six changes can be rung. A peal of four bells would ring four times as many changes as three, viz., 24; five bells five times as many as four, viz., 120; six bells six times as many as five, viz., 720; seven bells seven times as many as six, viz., 5040; and so on. It has

[1] Anglo-Saxon Chronicle, p. 500.

been calculated that it would take ninety-one years to ring the changes upon twelve bells at the rate of twenty strokes per minute.[1]

Dedication of Churches.

Several of the churches in Holderness have, according to the late Rev. Canon Raine, both ancient and modern ascriptions; it is difficult to account for the change. The name of the patron saint of each church would be formally assigned to it at its consecration. If a church was rebuilt or altered in such a way as to render re-consecration necessary, it was then permissible to change the name of the patron saint. In some instances a church may have been dedicated to a particular saint, whilst an oratory or chapel connected with it may have had a special dedication to some other saint, hence the two ascriptions. Where two saints are mentioned in the original dedication they were probably conjoined, and it will generally be found that the saint with the most striking name usually displaced the other. Prior to the Reformation,

[1] Archæological Journal, 48, 59.

S. Peter and S. Paul were frequently associated; subsequently, however, in a most unexpected manner, S. Paul has been forgotten.[1]

In mediæval times, the country people assembled on the anniversary of the dedication of the church; religious people met together on the eve of the day of commemoration, and continued to watch and pray all night, but in lapse of time there was but little devotion at these meetings; they became gradually friendly gatherings, hawkers and pedlars began to attend them to sell their wares, and petty dealers of various kinds set up stalls and booths in the churchyard,[2] hence we may trace the origin of our country fairs and village feasts. These annual gatherings continued not in their original purity, but degenerated into drunkenness and rioting, until, becoming a great scandal to Christianity, they were suppressed by the Church. Feasts are still observed on the church dedication days in several villages in Holderness.

[1] Rev. Canon Raine. [2] Thompson's History of Swine.

CHAPTER II.

Inscriptions on the Church Bells in Holderness.

Rural Deanery of Hedon.

BILTON. (S. Peter.)
Old ascription S. Mary Magdalene.

Two bells.

Two small bells (modern) in a bell turret at the west end of the church.

No inscription or date on either bell.

BURSTWICK. (All Saints.)

One bell.

> "Rev. William Clarke, Vicar, Sanctitas Domino. Edward Ward and William Ingleby Churchwardens, 1817. James Harrison founder."

This bell has been probably substituted for an older one.

Robert Harrison, the inventor of the Chronometer, established a bell foundry at Barton-upon-Humber in the 18th century. James

Harrison, whose foundry was at Barrow-upon-Humber, would probably be a descendant of his.

BURTON PIDSEA. (S. Peter.)
Old ascription S. S. Peter and Paul.

Three bells.

1. "God Be Our Good Speed T.S. 16 a.g. 77."
2. "John Mitchinson and Samuel Nightingale Churchwardens 16 a.g. 77."
3. "Andreas Gurney Fecit me et Duos alios Honeste 16 + 77."
    (Andrew Gurney worthily made me and two others 1677.)

The initials T.S. are probably those of a Sellers of York. The family of Sellers had bell foundries in York from 1662 to 1764, a.g. anno gratiæ.

Andrew Gurney was a bell-founder at Thetford.

These bells were re-cast in the year 1891, and consecrated by the Bishop of Hull (Dr. Blunt) 23rd December in the same year.

An ancient custom is said to have prevailed here of the parish clerk ringing the great bell every morning at four o'clock during the summer, and six during the winter, and at eight o'clock at night the year through. About the year 1782 this custom was relinquished by permission of the chief freeholders and other inhabitants at the request of the clerk.

EASINGTON. (ALL SAINTS.)

Three bells.

1. James Harrison of Barton, Founder, 1793.[1]
2. Rev. William Potchett, Vicar, John Fewson and John Stark Churchwardens. James Harrison, Barton, Founder.[1]
3. **Sancte Johannes Ora Pro nobis.**
    (Saint John pray for us.)

There is no date on this bell (3). The final s of nobis is reversed. The character of the letters is Lombardic, from that and the legend it is evidently a pre-Reformation bell.

ELSTERNWICK. (S. LAWRENCE.)

One bell.

LAVRENƆIVS EST NOMEN MEU STEPHANVS FRANKYS ME FIER.
(Lawrence is my name
Stephen Frankys caused me to be made).

[1] Vide Burstwick ante.

The letter C in Lavrencivs is reversed.

The final letters in "meu" and "fier" are obliterated; the correct reading doubtless is "meum" and "fieri fecit."

It is not clear whether Stephen Frankys was the donor or the founder of the bell, probably the donor. In 10 Richard II. (1396) lands in Hedon, Elsternwick and other places in Holderness were given by Robert Frankys, clerk to the prioress and convent of Killinge (Nunkeeling), for a chaplain to celebrate for Richard de Ravenser, Archdeacon of Lincoln, and John Frankeys, whilst they should live, and for their souls after they departed this life. And for the soul of Isabella, late Countess of Bedford, in the chapel of S. Lawrence of Elsternwick four days every week according to the ordination of the said Robert, etc.[1] Stephen Frankys would doubtless be a relative. There is no date on the bell, but the foregoing gives a clue to the date circa 1396. Isabella, Countess of Bedford, was the daughter of Edward III., and wife of Ingelram de Courcy, Earl of Bed-

[1] Poulson's History of Holderness, vol. ii, p. 74.

INSCRIPTIONS ON BELLS IN HOLDERNESS. 49

ford, who in right of his wife was Lord of the Seigniory of Holderness from 1356 to 1376. The countess died in 1377.

GARTON. (S. Michael.)

One bell.

The bell is hung close to the roof, the inscription, if any, cannot be discovered.

HALSHAM. (All Saints.)

Two bells.

1. + 𝔐aria 𝔐ater 𝔇ei miserere mei
   (Mary Mother of God have pity on me.)
2. + ihc est nomen meum.
   (Jesus is my name.)

The inscription seems to denote that it was a "Jesus" bell for the men as a comparison to a "Mary" bell for the women.

There is no date on either bell. The letters are of old English character, evidently pre-Reformation.

HEDON. (S. Augustine.)

Six bells.

1. Eustace Roper, Richard Gibson, Churchwardens, 1776.

2. Wind Them and Bringe Them and I will Ring for Them, 1687.
3. William and Philip Wightman made mee, 1686. The gvift of Charles Duncomb to the Corporation of Hedon in Yorkshire.
4. The same inscription.
5. The same inscription.
6. The gvift of Charles Duncomb to the Corporation of Hedon in Yorkshire, 1687. S. S. Ebor

There is no record to shew to which of the saints the church is dedicated. It is generally assumed that the dedication is to "Augustine," Bishop of Hippo.

The letters on the first bell are partially obliterated. The legend on the second bell, cast round the bell in basso relievo, near the crown, is probably intended for the Passing or Burial bell, and it may also have reference to the Marriage bell, thus: to the mourners "wind them (put on the winding sheet) and bring them (to the church for burial), and I will ring (knoll) for them. To the lovers, wind (win) them and bring them (to the church to be married), and I will ring (merrily) for them. The founder's name on the 3rd, 4th, and 5th

INSCRIPTIONS ON BELLS IN HOLDERNESS. 51

bells is cast round the bells in the same way. The name of the donor appears on the face of each of these bells about middle way between the skirt and the crown. On the 6th bell, the name of the donor appears round the bell, near the crown. Amidst a border of small bells and leaves, cast round the bell, is a shield between every two, bearing the letters $^{S.\ S.}_{Ebor,}$ the initials S. S. are those of Samuel Smith, of the City of York (Ebor), an eminent bell founder. Mr. Smith was the nephew of Mr. Gells, of York, whom Thoresby calls " the famousest painter of glass perhaps in the world." William and Philip Wightman were bell founders in London from 1682 to 1702. Sir Charles Duncomb was elected one of the representatives in Parliament for the Borough of Hedon in 1685. John Frankys, of Hedon, merchant, by his will dated 28th August, 1391, gave—

> "fabrica ecclesiæ S. Aug: & ad unam campanam ecclesiæ de Hedon Cs."

A set of hand-bells, thirty-seven in number, was presented to the church in July, 1874, by the Rev. Charles Edward Camidge, M.A.,

Rector of Wheldrake, for five years Vicar of Hedon, on condition that they be reserved for the sole use of the Hedon ringers for ever; that the governor for the time being have the charge of them, and report once in every three months to the churchwardens on their condition; and that the wardens undertake on behalf of themselves and their successors to maintain the same in due repair and tune.[1]

HILSTON. (S. Margaret.)

One bell.

Gloria Iu Altissimis Deo. 1713.
(Glory to God in the highest.)
E. Seller
Ebor

The letter "n" in "In" is reversed. Edward Seller was a bell founder at York; he was city sheriff in 1803.

HOLLYM. (S. Nicholas.)

Old ascription S. Catherine.

Two bells.

These bells were recently re-cast. There is no inscription on either of them.

---

[1] Table of benefactions in the church.

HOLMPTON. (S. Nicholas.)

One bell.

The bell is a very small and modern one.

HUMBLETON. (S. Peter.)

Old ascription S. S. Peter and Paul.

Three bells.

1. Venite Exvltemvs Domino 1700.
(Come, let us heartily rejoice in the Lord.)

    An. Slater   Church   S   S. S. 1
    Tho. Owbridge   Warden   Ebor

2. On Saboth Al To Church We call.
Peter Tympern, Ben. Hardy, a.g. 1676 Church Ward.

3. Vt Tvba sic sonitu Domini condvco cohortes.
(As with the sound of a trumpet I bring together the hosts of the Lord.)
RM. TH. RR. BB. TS. GL. IB. 1594.

The letters R.M. are probably the initials of the bell founder. Robert Merston was an itinerant at this time. T.H., Thomas Hall was vicar from 1592 to 1606. The other letters probably represent the then churchwardens.

KEYINGHAM. (S. Nicholas.)

Three bells.

1. James Harrison, Founder, Bart.,[2] 1819.[3]
2. & 3. 1819.[3]

[1] Vide Hedon ante.   [2] Barton-upon-Humber   [3] Vide Burstwick ante.

KILNSEA. (S. Helen.)

No bell.

The old church was washed away by the sea in 1826. For some time previous to the destruction of the church, the bell was removed and hung upon a tree to avoid the danger of bringing down the tower by the vibration of the bell when rung. The present church was built in 1865, when the old bell was sold, and has not since been replaced.

MARFLEET. (S. Giles.)

(Now in the Rural Deanery of Kingston-upon-Hull.)

One bell.

James Harrison, of Barton, Founder, 1794.[1]

OTTRINGHAM. (S. Wilfrid.)

Three bells.

1. Venite Exvltemvs Domino 1699   S. S. Ebor [2]
(Come, let us heartily rejoice in the Lord.)
2. Gloria In Altissimis Deo 1699   S. S. Ebor [2]
(Glory to God in the highest.)
3. Clangore Dvlcissimo Psallam Tibi Devs 1699   S. S. Ebor [2]
(With sweetest sound will I play to Thee, O Lord.)

[1] Vide Burstwick ante.   [2] Vide Hedon ante.

INSCRIPTIONS ON BELLS IN HOLDERNESS. 55

OWTHORNE. (S. Peter.)

Owthorne Church fell into the sea in 1816, and the bell was probably removed to Rimswell in 1819.

A chapel of ease to the church of Rimswell was built at Owthorne in 1850, which has a small bell without any inscription.

PATRINGTON. (S. Patrick.)

Five bells.

1. God Save The King 1674. G + O
2. . . . Christopher . . . Church-Wardens.
3. + Agreed on at Patrengton to cast thes bells by Samvel Proud. T. Hildyard.
   Wardens, E. Webster, T. Bvrton, I. Dalton, E. Smith, I. Pickard, 1674. G + O
4. In well and wo laud es Deo.
   (In well and woe praise God.)
   zyxwvtsrqponmlkihgfedcba.
5. John Taylor & Son, Founders, Loughborough, late of St. Neots, Oxford, and Buckland, Brewer, Devon, 1846.

The letters G + O on the 1st and 3rd bells are probably the initials of the bell founder, George Oldfield, of Nottingham. Oldfields, of Nottingham, were well-known bell founders at this time.

The inscription on the 2nd bell is partly illegible. The churchwardens in 1768 were Thomas Harrison and Christopher Bell. On the 3rd bell the letter "S" is reversed in every instance. Rev. Samuel Proud was Rector from 1660 to 1683. Captain Robert Hildyard, who died in June, 1685, and was buried in Beverley Minster, by his will left seventy pounds, half the interest "to repair the bell frames," and the other half to the poor on the 2nd day of October for ever. On the 4th bell the letters represent all the letters of the alphabet transposed.

PAULL. (S. Andrew.)
Modern ascription S. Andrew and S. Mary.

One bell.

James Harrison, Founder, Barrow, 1788.[1]

PRESTON. (All Saints.)

Three bells.

1. +Ut Tuba sic sonitu Domini conduco cohortes. Ano Dom 1662 W S
   (As a trumpet so with my Sound I assemble together the hosts of the Lord.)

[1] Vide Burstwick ante.

INSCRIPTIONS ON BELLS IN HOLDERNESS.

2. + 𝔐𝔞𝔯𝔪𝔞𝔡𝔲𝔠𝔲𝔰 𝔖𝔪𝔦𝔱𝔥, 𝔉𝔯𝔞𝔫𝔠𝔦𝔰𝔠𝔲𝔰 𝔗𝔲𝔯𝔫𝔥𝔬𝔩𝔪𝔢, 𝔊𝔲𝔞𝔯𝔡𝔦𝔞𝔫𝔦 𝔈𝔠𝔠𝔩𝔢𝔰𝔦𝔞𝔢. 𝔄𝔫𝔬 𝔇𝔬𝔪 1662 𝔚 𝔖

3. Gloria In Excelsis Deo, 1696.   S. S. Ebor [1]
   (Glory to God on high.)
   Ra. Burnsall, Wil. Winder, Gvardiani.

The letters on the 1st and 2nd bells are old English. A memorandum found amongst some papers relating to the church states that, " In 4th Eliz., the bells were taken out of this church and exported, that the ship wherein the bells were, when she was clear of Humbre and launched into the sea, being under sail, she, yet within sight, was seen to sink down into the sea, like that of Arthur Bulkley, 38th Bishop of Bangor, who for the like sacrilege was struck blind." W.S., the initials of William Sellers, of the City of York, bell founder, the father of Edward Sellers, vide Hilston ante.

RIMSWELL. (S. Mary.)

One bell.

Re-cast by John Warner & Sons, 1864 patent.
Jesus be our speed.
PHW. JN. FC. RB. JP. WH. 1630.

1 Vide Hedon ante.

This is no doubt the bell which formerly was in Owthorne Church; it would be removed to Rimswell when Owthorne Church fell into the sea in 1816. The initials on the bell, "P H W," are those of Paul Henzel Wilton, Vicar; "J N," those of John Newby, Curate; "F C," Francis Clappinson, South Frodingham; "R B," Robert Burnham, Rimswell; "J P," John Pybus, Owthorne; "W H," William Harrison, Waxholme; the churchwardens of the respective townships in the parish.

John Warner & Sons, bell founders, London.

ROOS. (ALL SAINTS.)

Three bells.

1. Venite exvltemvs Domino 1665. ss.[1]
(Come, let us heartily rejoice in the Lord.)
PK.   AR.   Church Wardens

2. Gloria In Altissimis Deo 1700   S. S. I Ebor
(Glory to God in the highest.)

3. Pacio Crventos Andreas Gvrney me Fecit.
(I pacify the cruel. Andrew Gurney made me.)[2]
NL. J^A. Thet. WM. CU. 1676

Although "Pacio Cruentos" is the correct reading on the bell, it is evidently a mistake;

---

[1] Vide Hedon ante.   [2] Vide Burton Pidsea ante.

it should be "Paco Cruentos" from the line "Excito lentos, dissipo ventos, paco cruentos."[1]

P.K., A.R., Paul Kitchin and Anthony Richardson were the churchwardens.[2]

A small sanctus bell was hung in the turret over the chancel arch in 1897, as a memorial of the Queen's Diamond Jubilee, bearing the inscription, I.H.S. 1897.

SKEFFLING. (S. Helen.)

Two bells.

1. James Harrison, Bell Founder, 1792.[3]
2. Tempus Edax Rervm.
   (Time is a destroyer of all things.)
   MS. Elizabeth Holme. MW. 1692.

Mrs. Elizabeth Holme was probably the donor of the bell.

M.W., William Mackereth was at this time vicar.

SPROATLEY. (S. Swithun.)

Two bells.

1. +*CAMPANA BEATI SVVITHVINI.*
   (The bell of the blessed Swithun.)

---

1 Vide page 1 ante.   2 Canon Machell's Roos Registers.
3 Vide Burstwick ante.

2. + *CAMPANA BEATI MARIE. I.K.*
(The bell of the blessed Mary.)

The initials " I. K." indicate that these bells were cast by John de Kirkham, an eminent bell founder at York in the latter part of the 14th century. The fabric rolls of York Minster for the year 1371 contain notices of dealings with " Johannes de Kirkham " in relation to the Minster bells.[1] The letter " N " is reversed in every instance on both bells. In 1888, on the restoration of the church, a set of tubular bells, the gift of the Rector (Rev. Charles Joseph Wall), was placed in the tower of the church, provided by Harrington & Co., of Coventry.

SUNK ISLAND. (HOLY TRINITY.)

One bell. No inscription (modern).

SUTTON. (S. JAMES.)
(Now in the Rural Deanery of Kingston-upon-Hull.)

Six bells. There were originally three bells.

---

[1] Church Bells in Leatham-Ward, by Rev. Henry Whitehead.

INSCRIPTIONS ON BELLS IN HOLDERNESS. 61

1. & 2. 1795.
3. Rev. George Thompson, Minister. Matthew Spencer & Thomas Eubank, Churchwardens.

1795.
James Harrison, of Barton, Founder of the peal.[1]

Miss Liddell, of Sutton, gave a new peal of six bells to the church in 1890. The three old bells were melted down, and the metal used in making a new peal. There is no inscription on any of the new bells. A brass plate in the church states that the bells were placed by Miss D. I. Liddell in memory of her brother.

THORNGUMBALD. (S. MARY.)

One bell.

A small modern bell in a bell turret at the west end of the church; no inscription or date.

TUNSTALL. (ALL SAINTS.)

Two bells.

1. + trinitate sacra fiat bec campana beata ibc.
   (By the sacred Trinity may this bell be blessed.)

---

[1] Vide Burstwick ante.

2. +*JOHES FRANKYS ME FECIT IN HONORE SCI AUGUSTINI.*
(John Frankys made me in honour of St. Augustine.)[1]

The bells have no date on them.

WELWICK. (S. Mary.)

One bell.

Est Campana Jesvs Maribus Dans Optime Plavsvs.
(This a bell telling forth to men most beautifully the praises of Jesus.)

There has probably been a Mary bell as well. A free rendering of the legend

"A Jesus bell
To men I tell
His praises well."[2]

+WK. TC. C Wards 16 ag 76 Tho. Crathorne SP.

Mr. Crathorne was a considerable landowner in the parish.

WINESTEAD. (S. Germanus.)

One bell.

Johannes Evangelista.
(John the Evangelist.)

The bell is fixed in a receptacle on the west wall; old characters.

[1] Vide Elsternwick and Hedon ante.   [2] Rev. Canon Maddock.

INSCRIPTIONS ON BELLS IN HOLDERNESS. 63

WITHERNSEA. (S. Nicholas.)

Five bells.

    1. A.D., 1894. Funds for these bells raised by ladies of Withernsea. Lavs Deo.
    2. 3. 4. 5. No inscriptions.

Rural Deanery of Hornsea.

ALDBOROUGH. (S. Bartholomew.)

Three bells.

    1. Stephanus Geere, Vicar, vehemens et S. Bartholomew vox qvasi Tuba. ivs 1664 ss.[1]
    (Stephen Geere, vicar of vehement zeal, and Saint Bartholomew, whose tone is as clear as a trumpet. Jesus.)
    2. + Maria virgo peperit christum.
    (The Virgin Mary brought forth Christ.)
    3. SOLI DEO GLORIA 1635 LJ. wo. ih. RH.
    (To God alone the Glory.)

Stephen Geere was instituted Vicar 7th December, 1660; Patron, Charles II. The letters on the 2nd bell are old English. On the 3rd bell, the letter " E " in " L. E." is reversed. The initials " W. O." are those of the bell founder, William Oldfield, of York.

    1 Vide Hedon ante.

ATWICK. (S. Peter.)
Modern ascription S. Lawrence.

Two bells.

1. No inscription.
2. + CѴMPѴNѴ IN HONORE SANCTI PETRI.
   (A bell in honour of Saint Peter.)

The letters are Lombardic. The letter "A" in Campana is reversed.

BARMSTON. (All Saints.)
(Now in the Rural Deanery of Bridlington.)

One bell.

Gloria In Altissimis Deo 1731.
(Glory to God in the highest.)

BEEFORD. (S. Leonard.)

Three bells.

1. *JHESVS BE OVR SPEDE* 1599 H + O
2. God save the Church, ovr Qveene, and Realme, and send us peace in Christ h + o Amen 1599.
3. Gloria Iu Excelsis Deo 1675.
   (Glory to God ou high.)
   TH. IS$^{Church}_{Wardeu}$S $^{S. S. 1}_{Ebor}$

The letters on the 1st bell are Lombardic. The letters h + o the initials of the bell founder,

1 Vide Hedon ante.

Henry Oldfield, Nottingham. On the 3rd bell the letter "n" in every case is reversed.

BRANDESBURTON. (S. Mary.)

Two bells.

    1. C. R. R. 1754.
    2. *CAMPANA DE BRANDESBURT. ECCE ANCILLA DOMINI ETC.*
    (The bell of Brandesburton. Behold the handmaid of the Lord, etc.)

·The initials C. R. R., Charles Richardson, Rector. The letters on the 2nd bell are Lombardic.

CATWICK. (S. Michael.)

Two bells.

There is no date on either bell, evidently pre-Reformation.

    1. *CAMPANA JHESU CRISTI + THOMAS DEKUN ME FECIT.*
    (The bell of Jesus Christ Thomas Dekun made me.)
    2. *AUE MARIA GRACIA PLENA.*
    (Hail Mary full of Grace.)

There is no date on either bell, evidently pre-Reformation.[1]

---

[1] Vide Halsham ante.

DUNNINGTON. (S. Nicholas.)

One bell.

No inscription.

NORTH FRODINGHAM. (S. Elgin.)
(Now in the Rural Deanery of Harthill.)

Three bells.

1. Rev. George H. Paul, Vicar.
   Edmund Julian & John Dent, **Church-wardens.**
   James Harrison, of Barton, Founder, 1794.[1]
2. Jesvs Be Ovr Speed, 1627. TI. WW.
3. James Harrison, of Barton, Founder, 1795.[1]

The letters W.W. are probably the initials of William Wakefield, bell founder.

GOXHILL. (S. Giles.)

One bell.

I.C., with the crest of Constable, of Wassand.

The initials I.C., probably those of John Constable, of Catfoss, who died 28th September, 1659.

HORNSEA. (S. Nicholas.)

Three bells.

1. (Tenor) Soli Deo Gloria 1634.
   (Glory be to God alone.)

[1] Vide Burstwick ante.

2. Robert Cotes, Vicar.   William Whytehead, Curate, 1767.
3. John Prudom, James Moor, William Wilson, John Bedell, Churchwardens, 1767.

LEVEN. (S. Faith.)

Four bells.

All have the same inscription :—

C. & G. Mears, Founders, London, 1845.

There were two bells in the tower of the old church (pulled down in 1845), one of them had on it the letters "MCL," which, it has been suggested, indicates the date 1150. The smaller bell marked MCL weighed 1 cwt., 4 stones. The larger one, dated 1664, had inscribed "venite exultemus Domino." These two bells were sent to London, and the present four new ones were supplied. The letters MCL must not, however, be taken to indicate the date. Pre-Reformation bells do not as a rule bear any date.

LISSET. (S. James.)

Two bells.

1. WOOrIIII.
2. No inscription.

MAPLETON. (All Saints.)

One bell.

> Cantemus Domino, 1708.
> (Let us sing unto the Lord.)
> George Carter, Curate, Durance Hodgson, Clark,
> Phineas Binns, Thomas Hodgson, Robt. Brankley,
> Robt. Lorimer, Church Wardens.

Copy of an old memorandum in the possession of Mr. Ake, joiner, Mapleton (1895).

> "December 15th, A.D., 1708. Mapleton bell being cracked was thrown out of ye north window of ye steepel, and was sent to York to be re-cast, weighing aboute a leaven 100 weight. Ye bell coming back from casting 15th daye of Aprill, 1709, was hung up again on ye 2nd day of June, being Ascension Day, weaying aboute eight 100 weight. Due to Bell founder, £05 03 09. For hanging ye bell, 00l 15s 0d. For working at ye same, 01s 6d, and five pence more. George Carter, Vicar, Phineas Binns, Robert Brankley, Thomas Hodgson, Clark. June ye 2nd, Anno, 1709."

NUNKEELING. (S. Helena.)

One bell.

The bell supposed to be an old one is not accessible.

RISE. (S. Mary.)
(Modern ascription, All Saints'.)

Three bells.

All the three bells are modern, and have the same inscription :—

"C. & G. Mears, Founders, London, 1845."

RISTON. (S. Margaret.)

Two bells.

1. *SANCTA MARGARETA ORA PRO NOBIS.*
   (Holy Margaret pray for us.)
2. Soli Deo Gloria, 1665   ss [2]
   (Glory be to God alone.)
   Timothie Rhodes, Rector.   HW CW TV Churchwardens.

ROUTH. (All Saints.)

One bell.

    Gloria Iu Altissimis Deo, 1732
    (Glory to God in the highest.)
        E. Seller [2]
        Ebor.

The letter "n" in In is reversed.

SIGGLESTHORNE. (S. Lawrence.)

Three bells.

All three bells have the same inscription :—

James Harrison, Bell Founder, Barrow, 1785.   J. H.[3]

---

[1] Vide Hedon ante.   [2] Vide Hilston ante.   [3] Vide Burstwick ante.

SKIPSEA. (ALL SAINTS.)

Three bells.

1. Venite exvltemvs Domino, 1676
   (Come let us heartily rejoice ni the Lord.)
   C.F. I.I. T.D. W.I. Churchwardens S. S. 1 Ebor
2. Gloria In Altissimis Deo, 1695
   (Glory to God in the highest.)
   Ralph Bainton Church Warden S. S. 1 Ebor
3. C. & G. Mears, Founders, London, 1845.

SOUTH SKIRLAUGH. (S. AUGUSTINE.)

Two bells.

1. Sabbata Pango + R + I + a.g., 1678.
   (I proclaim the Sabbath.)
2. Soli Deo Gloria Pax Hominibus, a.g., 1678.
   (Glory to God alone, peace to men.)

The letters R + I, the initials of Richard Ion, bell founder.

SWINE. (S. MARY.)

Four bells.

1. Rev. Matthew Williamson, Vicar. James Harrison of Barton, Founder. William Raines and Thomas Turner, Churchwardens, 1800.
2. 3. 4. The other three bells have all the same inscription.
   James Harrison of Barton, Founder, 1800.

1 Vide Hedon ante.

TICKTON. (S. Paul.)

One bell.

The bell is modern, circa 1845. No inscription.

ULROME. (S. Andrew.)

One bell.

    Gloria In Excelsis Deo, 1675.   S. S. Ebor [1]
    (Glory to God on high.)
        I. I.   Church Warden

WAGHEN. (S. Peter.)

Three bells.

1. Jesvs Be Ovr Speed, 1638.
2. The Lord Increas Ovr Faith. R.K. C.C. 1632.
3. *GOD SAVE HIS CHVRCH*, 1629, *W. W.*[2]

The bells were re-cast and re-hung on the restoration of the church in 1874.

WITHERNWICK. (S. Alban.)

Two bells.

No inscriptions.

Both these bells are modern. The old bell was sold on the restoration of the church in 1854.

   1 Vide Hedon ante.   2 Vide North Frodingham ante.

Dedication of Church Bells.

The following is the office for the dedication of church bells in the Diocese of York, as ordered by the Archbishop, and published by Mr. John Sampson, York:—

DEDICATION
OF
A PEAL OF BELLS.

¶ *The Bishop, with the Clergy, Choir, and Churchwardens, will enter the Tower.*

COLLECT.

PREVENT us, O Lord, in all our doings with Thy most gracious favour, and further us with Thy continual help; that in all our works begun, continued, and ended in Thee, we may glorify Thy holy Name, and finally by Thy mercy obtain everlasting life; through Jesus Christ our Lord. *Amen.*

¶ *The Churchwardens, taking the ropes of the Bells, shall then say—*

RIGHT Reverend Father in God, we request you to dedicate to the Glory of God, and the use of this Church, this peal of Bells.

¶ *The Bishop, receiving the ropes, shall then say—*

BY virtue of our sacred office, we do solemnly set apart and separate from all profane and unhallowed uses these Bells, now dedicated to the glory of God, for the benefit of His Holy Church.

INSCRIPTIONS ON BELLS IN HOLDERNESS.

¶ *Then delivering the ropes to the Vicar—*

Receive these Bells as a sacred trust, committed unto thee as the appointed Minister of Christ in this Church and Parish, and take heed that they be ever and only used in His Service and for His Glory.

¶ *After which the Bishop shall say to the Churchwardens and others standing by—*

You are to take notice that these Bells of the Church are committed to the custody of the Vicar of the Parish, to be used only with his consent, subject to the ultimate control of the Bishop of the Diocese.

¶ *The bells will then be chimed for a few minutes whilst the Bishop, Clergy, and Choir enter the Church.*

¶ *The Bishop shall then say—*

The Lord be with you.

And with thy Spirit.

Let us pray.

Our Father, &c.

O ALMIGHTY GOD, Who at the building of Thy Temple of old didst graciously receive the gifts of Thy faithful people, vouchsafe we beseech Thee to accept the offering of these Bells now provided by Thy servants for the use of this Church, and grant that as with a glad heart they have offered willingly, so they may ever rejoice before Thee with exceeding joy; through Jesus Christ our Lord. *Amen.*

GRANT, O Lord, that they who shall be appointed to use these Bells in the Service of Thy Church may ever do so with reverence and Godly fear, and keep themselves pure both in word and deed; for Jesus Christ's sake. *Amen.*

GRANT, O Lord, that all who shall be called by these Bells to Thy House of Prayer, may hear in them Thy loving invitation, and may so come unto Thee that they may find rest for their souls; through Thee and in Thee Who livest and reignest with the Father and the Holy Spirit, one God, world without end. *Amen.*

GRANT, O Lord, that all who are hindered, by sorrow or sickness or any other adversity, from assembling themselves together for Thy worship, may, by these Bells, be reminded, to their exceeding comfort, of the prayers of the Church, and may rejoice in the Communion of Saints, through Jesus Christ our Lord. *Amen.*

GRANT, O Lord, that all they, who in the midst of their worldly occupations shall hear the passing bell, may be warned to prepare for the time when they too shall depart from this life, and may learn so to number their days that they may apply their hearts unto wisdom, for the sake of Him who died for us and rose again, Jesus Christ our Lord. *Amen.*

HYMN OF THE OFFICE.

LIFTED safe within the steeple,
   Now our Bells are set on high,
To begin their holy mission,
   Midway 'twixt the earth and sky.
Far and near our hearts shall hear them,
   In our toil and in our rest,
Telling how in one communion
   Of one Church we all are blest.

When the birds sing early matins,
   And the God of Nature praise,
These their nobler morning music
   To the God of Grace shall raise.

And when evening shadows soften
    Cross and chancel, tower and aisle,
They shall blend their vesper summons
    With the day's departing smile.

When God's day of rest and gladness
    Calls us to our Father's home,
To His House and to His Altar
    They shall bid His children come:
They shall welcome little children
    Born of Water and the Word,
And their wedding chimes shall tell of
    Holier union with the Lord.

They shall comfort sick and dying
    In their hour of utmost need,
Whispering how, for weak and weary,
    Holy Church doth ever plead;
To the mourners they shall whisper
    That the dead in Christ are blest,
And our lost ones they shall welcome
    To their Father's loving breast.

Thus in joy and thus in sadness
    Shall our Bells 'twixt earth and sky
Lift our hearts from earth to heaven,
    Plead with man for God on high.
Consecrate them, Lord Jehovah,
    Holy may they be in Thee,
Whom we laud in adoration
    EVER BLESSED TRINITY. *Amen.*

Index.

Accession, Queen's, Bells rung on, 16, 39
Agnus bell, 14, 26
Aldborough bell inscriptions, 63
All Hallows Eve, 16; Festival, 39
Altar bell, 26
Angelus bell, 26, 32
Apprentices ringing the Pancake bell, 35
Archbishop's confirmation, Bells rung at, 41
Archdeacon's visitation, Bells rung at, 41
Atwick bell, 14; bell inscription, 64
Ave bell, 31

Baptism of bells, 7
Barmston bell inscriptions, 64
Bede, Venerable, 6
Beeford bell inscriptions, 64
Bell founders: Thomas Dekun, 65; Stephen Frankys, 48; Andrew Gurney, 46; Harrington & Co., 60; James Harrison, 45, 47, 53, 54, 56, 59, 61; Robert Harrison, 45; William Harrison, 58; John de Kirkham, 60; Mears & Co., 67, 69; Robert Merson, itinerant, 53; George Oldfield, 55; Henry Oldfield, 64; William Oldfield, 63; T. Sellers, 46; Edward Sellers, 52, 57; William Sellers, 57; Samuel Smith, 57; John Taylor & Sons, 55; William Wakefield, 66; Warner & Sons, 58; William and Philip Wightman, 51. Itinerant, 7

Bell-man, Perambulating, 18
Bells: Agnus, 26; Altar, 26; Angelus, 26; Ave, 31; Baptism of, 7; Benedictus, 9; censures by the Church, 12; chimed, When, 18; Consecration of, 9; Corse, 31; Curfew, 17, 33; Dates on, 15; exorcising powers, 10; Hand, 26, Harvest, 33; History of, 2; Howslynge, 30; Jesus, 9, 28; Legendary lore, 3; Litany, 24; Lyche, 31; Mary, 9; Marriage, 19; Mayor's, 24; Names of, 7; Passing, 19; Poor, 22; Pre-Reformation, 14; Present uses, 17; Priest's, 22; Protective character, 10; Rung, when to be, 18; Sacring, 26; Sanctus, 25; Saunce, 25; Sermon, 24; Small, 31; Soul's, 20; Thunderstorms, 11; Tickynge, 30; Tolled, when to be, 18
Berengarian controversy, 29
Bilton bell inscriptions, 45
Black letter character, 15
Blunt, Dr., Bishop of Hull, 10, 46
Brandesburton bell inscriptions, 65
Burstwick bell inscriptions, 45
Burton, Thomas, Abbot of Meaux, 9
Burton Pidsea, Consecration of bells at, 10; bell inscriptions, 46; ringing custom, 46

Camidge, Rev. C. E., gift of hand-bells to Hedon, 51
Campania, Bells invented in, 6

INDEX.

Catwick, Pre-Reformation bell at, 14; Jesus bell, 30; bell inscriptions, 65
Censures by the Church, Bells used in, 12
Change ringing, 42
Chaucer on swearing by the bell, 12
Christmas Day, 16, 37
Churches, Dedication of, 43
Civil War, Desecration of bells during, 13
Columba, Abbot, Use of bells on assembling to worship, 5
Confirmations, Bells rung at, 41
Consecration of bells, 9, 10
Coronation, Queen's, Bells rung at, 16, 39
Corse or Lyche bell, 31
Country fairs, Origin of, 44
Cox, Rev. Dr., 10n, 34n
Cumian, Abbot, his life of Columba, 5
Curfew bell, 17, 33

Dates on bells not observed till 16th century, 15
Dedication of bells, Office for, in the Diocese of York, 72
Dedication of churches, 43
Dekun, Thomas, bell founder, 65
Drake, Dr., on the New Year, 38
Du Cange on introduction of bells, 6
Duncomb, Sir Charles, donor of Hedon bells, 51
Dunnington bell inscriptions, 66
Dunstan, St., a skilful artificer, 6

Easington, Pre-Reformation bell at, 14; bell inscriptions, 47
Easter Monday, Bells rung, 14; choosing churchwardens, 38
Elsternwick, Pre-Reformation bell at, 14; bell inscriptions, 47-48
Elections, Parliamentary, Bells rung at, 41
Episcopal Visitations, Peal of bells at, 17, 41

Excommunication by bell, book, and candle, 12
Exorcising power of bells, 10
Eyre, Simon, Lord Mayor of London, institutes observance of Shrove Tuesday, 35

Fairs, country, Origin of, 44
Feasts, village, Origin of, 44; still observed in Holderness, 44
Flamborough, Perambulating bellman at, 18
Fletcher's work on Niniveh, 3n
Folkmote bell in S. Paul's Cathedral, 29
Fosbroke, 23n, 35
Frankys, John, 48, 51, 62
 ,, Robert, 48
 ,, Stephen, bell founder, 48
Frodingham, North, Harvest bell, 34; bell inscriptions, 66

Garton bell inscriptions, 49
Gatty, Rev. Dr., 1
Good Friday custom at Hedon, 38
Goulding, Baring, 11n
Gowrie Plot, 16, 40
Goxhill bell inscriptions, 66
Gregory IX., Pope, origin of Sanctus bell, 28
Gunpowder Plot, 16, 40
Gurney, Andrew, bell founder, 16, 40

Halifax rhyme on Pancake bell, 37
Halsham, Pre-Reformation bell at, 14; bell inscriptions, 49; Jesus bell, 49
Hames hudde, 30
Hand-bells, 30
Harrison, James, bell founder, 45, 47, 53, 54, 56, 59, 61
 ,, Robert, bell founder, 45
 ,, William, bell founder, 58
Harrington & Co., bell founders, 60

INDEX.   79

Harvest bell, 17, 33
Hedon bells, 23 ; bell inscriptions, 49 ; Audit days, bells rung on, 41 ; ringers paid by Corporation, 41 ; legends on bells, 19, 23 ; fees on ringing, 21 ; Poor bell, 21 ; hand-bells, 51
Hilston bell inscriptions, 62
History of bells, 2
Hollym bell inscriptions, 52
Holmpton bell inscriptions, 53
Hornsea bell inscriptions, 66
Howslinge bell, 30
Hull, Bishop of, 10, 46
,, S. Mary's, Great bell at, 22
Humbleton bell inscriptions, 53

Induction of a new incumbent, Bell rung on, 17, 41
,, of Vicar of Hedon (1676), 42
Inventarium Monumentorum Superstitionem, 13
Itinerant bell founders, 7

Jesus bell, 9, 28, 49, 62
Jewish Church, Bells not used in, 4
Jubilee, Queen's Diamond, bell at Roos, 59

Keyingham bell inscriptions, 53
Kilnsea bell inscription, 54
Kirkham, John de, bell founder, 60

Lake, Dr., Prebendary of York, 36
Legendary lore on bells, 3
Leven, Pre-Reformation bell at, 14 ; bell inscriptions, 67
Levites, Silver trumpets of, 3
Liddell, Miss J. D., donor of bells at Sutton, 61
Lissett bell inscriptions, 67
Litany bell, 24
Lombardic letters on bells, 15
London, Lord Mayor of, observance of Shrove Tuesday, 35
Lyche or Corse bell, 31

Machell, Rev. Canon, 59n
Maddock, Rev. Canon, 62n
Malmesbury Abbey, Peal of bells in, 6
Mapleton bell inscription, 68
Marriage bell, 19
Marfleet bell inscription, 54
Mary bell, 9
May-pole, 28
May games, 28
Mayor's bell, 24
Mayor choosing, Bells rung on, 17, 41
Mears, C. & G., bell founders, 67, 69
Meaux Abbey, Bells in, 9
Merson, Robert, itinerant bell founder, 53
Muffled bells, 23 ; custom at Hedon, 38

Names given to bells, 9
Noah, Invention of bells attributed to, 3
Nola, Bells invented in, 6
Nunkeeling bell inscriptions, 68

Office for dedication of bells in the Diocese of York, 72
Oldfield, George, bell founder, 55
,, Henry, bell founder, 64
,, William, bell founder, 63
Ottringham bell inscriptions, 54
Owthorne bell inscriptions, 55

Pancake bell, 17, 35
Patrington bell inscriptions, 55
Parliamentary elections, Peal of bells at, 17
Passing bell, 19
Patrick, S., distributed bells in Ireland, 5
Paull bell inscriptions, 56
Peacock, Edward, F.S.A., 13n, 26n, 28n, 30n
Perambulating bell-man, 18
Poor bell, 22
Pre-Reformation bells in Holderness, 14

INDEX.

Preston Harvest bell, 33; bell inscriptions, 56; legend, 57
Priest's bell, 24
Puritans, Removal of bells by, 13

Queen's Birthday peal of bells, 16, 39
,, Accession peal of bells, 16, 39
,, Coronation peal of bells, 16, 39

Raine, Rev. Canon, on dedication of churches, 43, 44*n*
Readhead, Robinson, 18*n*
Richmond Cathedral, Jesus bell in, 29
Rimswell bell inscriptions, 57
Rise bell inscriptions, 69
Riston, 14; bell inscriptions, 69
Roos bell inscriptions, 58; Diamond Jubilee bell, 59
Routh bell inscriptions, 69
Royal Oak Day, 16, 39

Sacring bell, 26
Sanctus bell, 25
Saunce bell, 25
Scarborough, William of, Abbot of Meaux, 9
Sellers, Edward, bell founder, 52, 57
,, T., bell founder, 46
,, William, bell founder, 57
Sermon bell, 24
Sex of deceased indicated by Passing bell, 22
Shrove Tuesday, Pancake bell rung on, 35
Sigglesthorne bell inscriptions, 69
Skeffling bell inscriptions, 59
Skipsea bell inscriptions, 70
Skirlaugh, South, bell inscriptions, 70
Small bells used by the Celtic missionaries, 31
Sproatley pre-Reformation bells, 14; bell inscriptions, 59; Rev. C. J. Wall, donor of bells, 60

Smith, Samuel, bell founder, 57
Soul bell, 20
Sunk Island bell inscriptions, 60
Sutton bell inscriptions, 60; gift of bells by Miss Liddell, 61
Swearing by the bell, 12
Swine bell inscriptions, 70

Tabernacle in the wilderness, Bells applied to, 3
Taylor, John, & Son, bell founders, 55
Thorngumbald bell inscriptions, 61
Thunderstorms, Bells used to dispel, 10
Tickton bell inscription, 71
Tickynge bell, 30
Tolled, Bells when to be, 18
Tuba Dei inscription, 3
Tunstall bell inscriptions, 61

Ulrome bell inscription, 71
Urban II., Pope, origin of Sanctus bell, 28

Vestry meetings, 38
Village feasts, Origin of, 44
Visitations, Archdeacon's, Bells rung on, 41

Waghen bell inscriptions, 71
Wakefield, William, bell founder, 66
Wall, Rev. Charles Joseph, donor of bells to Sproatley, 58
Warner & Sons, bell founders, 58
Welwick bell inscriptions, 62
Westminster, Guild of, 39
,, Great Bell, 39
Whitehead, Rev. Henry, Church Bells in Leatham Ward, 60*n*
Wightman, William & Philip, bell founders, 51
Winestead, 14; bell inscriptions, 62
Withernsea bell inscriptions, 63
Withernwick bell inscription, 71

York Diocese, Office for dedication of bells in, 72

Subscribers.

His Grace the Lord Archbishop of York, Bishopthorpe (2 copies).

Abraham, Rev. W. H., M.A., Hull.
Andrews, Mr. William, Hull (2 copies).
Askew, Mr. Francis, Blake Street, Hull.

Bathurst, The Right Rev. the Bishop of, Bishop's Court, Bathurst, New South Wales.
Beverley, The Right Rev. the Bishop of, Bolton Percy Rectory.
Bathe, Rev. Anthony, M.A., Fridaythorpe Vicarage.
Béal, Alderman, Hedon.
Bell, Mr. Edward, Preston.
Bethell, William, Esq., J.P., Rise Park (4 copies).
Blashill, Thos., Esq., Tavistock Square, London.
Booth, Haworth, Col., J.P., Hull Bank Hall.
Briscoe, J. Potter, Esq., F.R.H.S., Free Library, Nottingham.
Brown, W. K., Esq., Preston.
Brown, Mr. Walter, Savile Street, Hull.

Cust, Purey, Very Rev. A. P., D.D., Dean of York, Deanery, York.
Clements, Rev. Canon, M.A., Sub-Dean of Lincoln, Lincoln.
Cobby, Rev. William, M.A., Swine Vicarage (2 copies).
Cooper, Rev. J. N., M.A., Filey Vicarage.
Cooper, J. S., Esq., Parliament Street, Hull.

Dibb, Col., J.P., Kirk Ella, Hull.
Dix, Miss, Hedon.

Fairbank, T. H., Esq., M.P., London.
Foster, Miss, Hilston.

Galloway, Richard, Esq., Hull.

Hull, The Right Rev. the Bishop of, Scarborough Vicarage.
Hall, Councillor J. G., Lindum House, Berkley Street, Hull.
Harland, Thomas, Esq., Bridlington.
Hawksley, B. F., Esq., Hyde Park Gardens, London.
Hildyard, J. T., Esq., J.P., Cherry Burton (2 copies).
Hobart, Col., R.A., J.P., Grimston Garth.

SUBSCRIBERS.

Holden, Thos., Esq., London (2 copies).
Holmes, T. B., Esq., J.P., Hornsea.
Holmes, Mrs., Elsternwick Hall.

Isaacson, Rev. S., North Frodingham Vicarage.

Jackson, J. L., Esq., M.D., Hedon.
Johnson, Mr. T. B., Hedon (3 copies).
Judge, Major, Hull.

Kay, Rev. E. B., B.A., Vicar of Marfleet, Hedon.
Kelly, Rev. T. W., M.A., Mapleton Vicarage.

Lambert, Rev. J. M., LL.D., Rural Dean, Newland Vicarage.
Lucas, Rev. William, M.A., Burstwick Vicarage.

Morrill, Henry, Esq., Mayor of Hull.
Mabb, W. H., Esq., Patrington.
Machell, Rev. Canon, M.A., S. Martin's Vicarage, York.
Maddock, Rev. Canon, M.A., Rural Dean, Patrington Rectory.
Medcalf, Rev. William, M.A., Rural Dean, Leven Rectory.
Middlemiss, R., Esq., Linnæus Street, Hull.
Miller, Rev. J. N., M.A., Winestead Rectory.
Mills, James, Esq., Beverley.
Milner, Mr. Alfred, Subscription Library, Hull.
Milsome, Rev. Edward, M.A., Roos Rectory.
Morris, Rev. M. C., B.C.L., Nunburnholme Rectory.
Morrissy, F. W., Esq., Durham Street, Hull.

Nolloth, Rev. Canon, D.D., Rural Dean, Beverley.

Palmes, Ven. James, D.D., Archdeacon of the East Riding, Burton Agnes Rectory (2 copies).
Page, Mr. G. W. B., Spring Street, Hull.
Park, W. R., Esq., Catwick.
Park, Mrs., Market Hill, Hedon.
Park, Rev. G. E., B.A., Burton Fleming Vicarage.
Park, R. Alan, Esq., Hedon.
Pearson, Rev. W. J., L.T., Ardwicke Lodge, Hull.
Proctor, Mrs., Woodlands, Whitby.
Prole, Rev. A. B., Aldborough Vicarage.
Pugh, W. B., Esq., J.P., Patrington (2 copies).
Pudsey, Col. Fawcett, Crown Terrace, Hull.

Quilter, Rev H. K., M.A., Bilton Vicarage.

Readhead, Mr. Robinson, Flamborough.
Reeder, Mr. W. W., Queen Street, Hull.

SUBSCRIBERS.

Reynoldson, Thos., Esq., J.P., Whitefriargate, Hull.
Richardson, Rev. J. H., M.A., Hedon Vicarage.
Robinson, Rev. Alfred, B.A., Humbleton Vicarage.
Rowsell, Rev. Canon, M.A., Rural Dean, Topcliffe Vicarage.
Rylatt, Mr. W. H., Sculcoates, Hull.

Scriven, Rev. F. T., Roos.
Scott, Councillor, J.P., Hull.
Scott, F. A., Esq., Sutton.
Sherburne, John, Esq., The Park, Hull.
Shipton, Rev. P. M., LL.B., Halsham Rectory.
Smith, Rev. A. Hippisley, Langton Rectory.
Smith, Rev. Wm., Catwick Rectory.
Smith, Rev. D. J., Presbytery, Hedon (2 copies).
Sykes, Christopher, Esq., Mayfair, London (6 copies).
Symons, Alderman, Coltman Street, Hull.

Terry, Sir Joseph, Hawthorne Villa, York.
Thompson, John, Esq., Pocklington.
Todd, Mr. William, Hedon.
Todd, Mr. John, Leytonstone Road, London.
Travis-Cook, Major John, F.R.H.S., Hull.
Turner, Tom, Esq., Beverley.

Wade, J. E., Esq., J.P., Brantinghamthorpe.
Walton, F. F., Esq., Hull.
Watson, Rev. Canon, M.A., Residence, York.
Watson, James, Esq., Hedon.
Wellsted, Col., The Park, Hull.
West, B., Esq., Sutton.
West, T. H., Esq., Hedon (2 copies).
Westbrooke, Rev. W. F., M.A., Caistor Vicarage.
Wilson, E. S., Esq., Melton.
Woodhouse, Herbert, Esq., LL.D., Roos.

Young, James, Esq., Hull.

LIST OF PUBLICATIONS
OF
WILLIAM ANDREWS & CO.,
5, FARRINGDON AVENUE, LONDON.

The Church Treasury of History, Custom, Folk-Lore, etc.

Edited by WILLIAM ANDREWS f.r.h.s.

Demy 8vo., 7s. 6d. Numerous Illustrations.

Contents :—Stave-Kirks—Curious Churches of Cornwall—Holy Wells—Hermits and Hermit Cells—Church Wakes—Fortified Church Towers—The Knight Templars: their Churches and their Privileges—English Mediæval Pilgrimages—Pilgrims' Signs—Human Skin on Church Doors—Animals of the Church in Wood, Stone, and Bronze—Queries in Stones—Pictures in Churches—Flowers and the Rites of the Church—Ghost Layers and Ghost Laying—Church Walks—Westminster Wax-Works—Index.

"It is a work that will prove interesting to the clergy and churchmen generally, and to all others who have an antiquarian turn of mind, or like to be regaled occasionally by reading old-world customs and anecdotes."—*Church Family Newspaper.*

"Mr. Andrews has given us some excellent volumes of Church lore, but none quite so good as this. The subjects are well chosen. They are treated brightly and with considerable detail, and they are well illustrated. . . . . . Mr. Andrews is himself responsible for some of the most interesting papers, but all his helpers have caught his own spirit, and the result is a volume full of information well and pleasantly put."—*London Quarterly Review.*

"Those who seek information regarding curious and quaint relics or customs will find much to interest them in this book. The illustrations are good."—*Publishers' Circular.*

"An excellent and entertaining book."—*Newcastle Daily Leader.*

"The book will be welcome to every lover of archæological lore."—*Liverpool Daily Post.*

"The volume is of a most informing and suggestive character, abounding in facts not easy of access to the ordinary reader, and enhanced with illustrations of a high order of merit, and extremely numerous."—*Birmingham Daily Gazette.*

"The contents of the volume are very good."—*Leeds Mercury.*

"The volume is sure to meet with a cordial reception."—*Manchester Courier.*

"A fascinating book."—*Stockport Advertiser.*

"Mr. Andrews has brought together much curious matter."—*Manchester Guardian.*

"The book is a very readable one, and will receive a hearty welcome."—*Herts. Advertiser.*

"Mr. William Andrews has been able to give us a very acceptable and useful addition to the books which deal with the curiosities of Church lore, and for this deserves our hearty thanks. The manner in which the book is printed and illustrated also commands our admiration."—*Norfolk Chronicle.*

Antiquities and Curiosities of the Church.

Edited by WILLIAM ANDREWS, f.r.h.s.

Demy 8vo., 7s. 6d. Numerous Illustrations.

Contents :—Church History and Historians—Supernatural Interference in Church Building—Ecclesiastical Symbolism in Architecture—Acoustic Jars—Crypts—Heathen Customs at Christian Feasts—Fish and Fasting—Shrove-tide and Lenten Customs—Wearing Hats in Church—The Stool of Repentance—Cursing by Bell, Book, and Candle—Pulpits—Church Windows—Alms-Boxes and Alms-Dishes—Old Collecting Boxes—Gargoyles—Curious Vanes—People and Steeple Rhymes—Sun-Dials—Jack of the Clock-House—Games in Churchyards—Circular Churchyards—Church and Churchyard Charms and Cures—Yew Trees in Churchyards.

"A very entertaining work."—*Leeds Mercury.*

"A well-printed, handsome, and profusely illustrated work."—*Norfolk Chronicle.*

"There is much curious and interesting reading in this popular volume, which moreover has a useful index."—*Glasgow Herald.*

"The contents of the volume is exceptionally good reading, and crowded with out-of-the way, useful, and well selected information on a subject which has an undying interest."—*Birmingham Mercury.*

"In concluding this notice it is only the merest justice to add that every page of it abounds with rare and often amusing information, drawn from the most accredited sources. It also abounds with illustrations of our old English authors, and it is likely to prove welcome not only to the Churchman, but to the student of folk-lore and of poetical literature."—*Morning Post.*

"We can recommend this volume to all who are interested in the notable and curious things that relate to churches and public worship in this and other countries."—*Newcastle Daily Journal.*

"It is very handsomely got up and admirably printed, the letterpress being beautifully clear."—*Lincoln Mercury.*

"The book is well indexed."—*Daily Chronicle.*

"By delegating certain topics to those most capable of treating them, the editor has the satisfaction of presenting the best available information in a very attractive manner."—*Dundee Advertiser.*

"It must not be supposed that the book is of interest only to Churchmen, although primarily so, for it treats in such a skilful and instructive manner with ancient manners and customs as to make it an invaluable book of reference to all who are concerned in the seductive study of antiquarian subjects."—*Chester Courant.*

The Miracle Play in England,

An Account of the Early Religious Drama.

By SIDNEY W. CLARKE, Barrister-at-Law.

Crown 8vo., 3s. 6d. Illustrated.

In bygone times the Miracle Play formed an important feature in the religious life of England. To those taking an interest in the history of the Church of England, this volume will prove useful. The author has given long and careful study to this subject, and produced a reliable and readable book, which can hardly fail to interest and instruct the reader. It is a volume for general reading, and for a permanent place in the reference library.

Contents :—The Origin of Drama—The Beginnings of English Drama—The York Plays—The Wakefield Plays—The Chester Plays—The Coventry Plays—Other English Miracle Plays—The Production of a Miracle Play—The Scenery, Properties, and Dresses—Appendix—The Order of the York Plays—Extract from City Register of York, 1426—The Order of the Wakefield Plays—The Order of the Chester Plays—The Order of the Grey Friars' Plays at Coventry—A Miracle Play in a Puppet Show—Index.

"Mr. Clarke has chosen a most interesting subject, one that is attractive alike to the student, the historian, and the general reader .... A most interesting volume, and a number of quaint illustrations add to its value."—*Birmingham Daily Gazette.*

"The book should be useful to many."—*Manchester Guardian.*

"An admirable work."—*Eastern Morning News.*

"Mr. Sidney Clarke's concise monograph in 'The Miracle Play in England' is another of the long and interesting series of antiquarian volumes for popular reading issued by the same publishing house. The author briefly sketches the rise and growth of the 'Miracle' or 'Mystery' play in Europe and in England ; and gives an account of the series or cycle of these curious religious dramas—the forerunners of the modern secular play—performed at York, Wakefield, Chester, Coventry, and other towns in the middle ages. But his chief efforts are devoted to giving a sketch of the manner of production, and the scenery, properties, and dresses of the old miracle play, as drawn from the minute account books of the craft and trade guilds and other authentic records of the period. Mr. Clarke has gone to the best sources for his information, and the volume, illustrated by quaint cuts, is an excellent compendium of information on a curious byeway of literature and art."—*The Scotsman.*

Historic Dress of the Clergy.

BY THE REV. GEO. S. TYACK, B.A.,

Author of "The Cross in Ritual, Architecture, and Art."

Crown, cloth extra, 3s. 6d.

The work contains thirty-three illustrations from ancient monuments, rare manuscripts, and other sources.

"A very painstaking and very valuable volume on a subject which is just now attracting much attention. Mr. Tyack has collected a large amount of information from sources not available to the unlearned, and has put together his materials in an attractive way. The book deserves and is sure to meet with a wide circulation."—*Daily Chronicle.*

"This book is written with great care, and with an evident knowledge of history. It is well worth the study of all who wish to be better informed upon a subject which the author states in his preface gives evident signs of a lively and growing interest."—*Manchester Courier.*

"Those who are interested in the Dress of the Clergy will find full information gathered together here, and set forth in a lucid and scholarly way."—*Glasgow Herald.*

"We are glad to welcome yet another volume from the author of 'The Cross in Ritual, Architecture, and Art.' His subject, chosen widely and carried out comprehensively, makes this a valuable book of reference for all classes. It is only the antiquary and the ecclesiologist who can devote time and talents to research of this kind, and Mr. Tyack has done a real and lasting service to the Church of England by collecting so much useful and reliable information upon the dress of the clergy in all ages, and offering it to the public in such a popular form. We do not hesitate to recommend this volume as the most reliable and the most comprehensive illustrated guide to the history and origin of the canonical vestments and other dress worn by the clergy, whether ecclesiastical, academical, or general, while the excellent work in typography and binding make it a beautiful gift-book."—*Church Bells.*

"A very lucid history of ecclesiastical vestments from Levitical times to the present day."—*Pall Mall Gazette.*

"The book can be recommended to the undoubtedly large class of persons who are seeking information on this and kindred subjects."—*The Times.*

"The work may be read either as pastime or for instruction, and is worthy of a place in the permanent section of any library. The numerous illustrations, extensive contents table and index, and beautiful workmanship, both in typography and binding, are all features of attraction and utility."—*Dundee Advertiser.*

The Cross in Ritual, Architecture, and Art.

By the REV. GEO. S. TYACK, B.A.

Crown 8vo., 3s. 6d. Numerous Illustrations.

THE AUTHOR of this Volume has brought together much valuable and out-of-the-way information which cannot fail to interest and instruct the reader. The work is the result of careful study, and its merits entitle it to a permanent place in public and private libraries. Many beautiful illustrations add to the value of the Volume.

"This book is reverent, learned, and interesting, and will be read with a great deal of profit by anyone who wishes to study the history of the sign of our Redemption."—*Church Times.*

"A book of equal interest to artists, archæologists, architects, and the clergy has been written by the Rev. G. S. Tyack, upon 'The Cross in Ritual, Architecture, and Art.' Although Mr. Tyack has restricted himself to this country, this work is sufficiently complete for its purpose, which is to show the manifold uses to which the Cross, the symbol of the Christian Faith, has been put in Christian lands. It treats of the Cross in ritual, in Church ornament, as a memorial of the dead, and in secular mason work; of preaching crosses, wayside and boundary crosses, well crosses, market crosses, and the Cross in heraldry. Mr. Tyack has had the assistance of Mr. William Andrews, to whom he records his indebtedness for the use of his collection of works, notes, and pictures; but it is evident that this book has cost many years of research on his own part. It is copiously and well illustrated, lucidly ordered and written, and deserves to be widely known."—*Yorkshire Post.*

"This is an exhaustive treatise on a most interesting subject, and Mr. Tyack has proved himself to be richly informed and fully qualified to deal with it. All lovers of ecclesiastical lore will find the volume instructive and suggestive, while the ordinary reader will be surprised to find that the Cross in the churchyard or by the roadside has so many meanings and significances. Mr. Tyack divides his work into eight sections, beginning with the pre-Christian cross, and then tracing its development, its adaptations, its special uses, and applications, and at all times bringing out clearly its symbolic purposes. We have the history of the Cross in the Church, of its use as an ornament, and of its use as a public and secular instrument; then we get a chapter on 'Memorial Crosses,' and another on 'Wayside and Boundary Cross.' The volume teems with facts, and it is evident that Mr. Tyack has made his study a labour of love, and spared no research in order, within the prescribed limits, to make his work complete. He has given us a valuable work of reference, and a very instructive and entertaining volume."—*Birmingham Daily Gazette.*

"An engrossing and instructive narrative."—*Dundee Advertiser.*

"As a popular account of the Cross in history, we do not know that a better book can be named."—*Glasgow Herald.*

"Mr. Andrews' books are always interesting."—*Church Bells.*

"No student of Mr. Andrews' books can be a dull after-dinner speaker, for his writings are full of curious out-of-the-way information and good stories."—*Birmingham Daily Gazette.*

England in the Days of Old.

By WILLIAM ANDREWS, F.R.H.S.,

Demy 8vo., 7s. 6d. Numerous Illustrations.

THIS volume is one of unusual interest and value to the lover of olden days and ways, and can hardly fail to interest and instruct the reader. It recalls many forgotten episodes, scenes, characters, manners, customs, etc., in the social and domestic life of England.

CONTENTS :—When Wigs were Worn—Powdering the Hair—Men Wearing Muffs—Concerning Corporation Customs—Bribes for the Palate—Rebel Heads on City Gates—Burial at Cross Roads—Detaining the Dead for Debt—A Nobleman's Household in Tudor Times—Bread and Baking in Bygone Days—Arise, Mistress, Arise!—The Turnspit—A Gossip about the Goose—Bells as Time-Tellers—The Age of Snuffing—State Lotteries—Bear-Baiting—Morris Dancers—The Folk-Lore of Midsummer Eve—Harvest Home—Curious Charities—An Old-Time Chronicler.

LIST OF ILLUSTRATIONS :—The House of Commons in the time of Sir Robert Walpole—Egyptian Wig—The Earl of Albemarle—Campaign Wig—Periwig with Tail—Ramillie-Wig—Pig-tail Wig—Bag-Wig—Archbishop Tilotson—Heart-Breakers—A Barber's Shop in the time of Queen Elizabeth—With and Without a Wig—Stealing a Wig—Man with Muff, 1693—Burying the Mace at Nottingham—The Lord Mayor of York escorting Princess Margaret—The Mayor of Wycombe going to the Guildhall—Woman wearing a Scold's Bridle—The Brank—Andrew Marvell—Old London Bridge, shewing heads of rebels on the gate—Axe, Block, and Executioner's Mask—Margaret Roper taking leave of her father, Sir Thomas More—Rebel Heads, from a print published in 1746—Temple Bar in Dr. Johnson's time—Micklegate Bar, York—Clock, Hampton Court Palace—Drawing a Lottery in the Guildhall, 1751—Advertising the Last State Lottery—Partaking of the Pungent Pinch—Morris Dance, from a painted window at Betley—Morris Dance, temp. James I.—A Whitsun Morris Dance—Bear Garden, or Hope Theatre, 1647—The Globe Theatre, temp. Elizabeth—Plan of Bankside early in the Seventeenth Century—John Stow's Monument.

A carefully prepared Index enables the reader to refer to the varied and interesting contents of the book.

"A very attractive and informing book."—*Birmingham Daily Gazette.*

"Mr. Andrews has the true art of narration, and contrives to give us the results of his learning with considerable freshness of style, whilst his subjects are always interesting and picturesque."—*Manchester Courier.*

"The book is of unusual interest."—*Eastern Morning News.*

"Of the many clever books which Mr. Andrews has written none does him greater credit than "England in the Days of Old," and none will be read with greater profit."—*Northern Gazette.*

Legal Lore: Curiosities of Law and Lawyers.

Edited by WILLIAM ANDREWS, f.r.h.s.

Demy 8vo., Cloth extra, 7s. 6d.

Contents:—Bible Law—Sanctuaries—Trials in Superstitious Ages—On Symbols—Law Under the Feudal System—The Manor and Manor Law—Ancient Tenures—Laws of the Forest—Trial by Jury in Old Times—Barbarous Punishments—Trials of Animals—Devices of the Sixteenth Century Debtors—Laws Relating to the Gipsies—Commonwealth Law and Lawyers—Cock-Fighting in Scotland—Cockieleerie Law—Fatal Links—Post-Mortem Trials—Island Laws—The Little Inns of Court—Obiter.

"There are some very amusing and curious facts concerning law and lawyers. We have read with much interest the articles on Sanctuaries, Trials in Superstitious Ages, Ancient Tenures, Trials by Jury in Old Times, Barbarous Punishments, and Trials of Animals, and can heartily recommend the volume to those who wish for a few hours' profitable diversion in the study of what may be called the light literature of the law."—*Daily Mail.*

"Most amusing and instructive reading."—*The Scotsman.*

"The contents of the volume are extremely entertaining, and convey not a little information on ancient ideas and habits of life. While members of the legal profession will turn to the work for incidents with which to illustrate an argument or point a joke, laymen will enjoy its vivid descriptions of old-fashioned proceedings and often semi-barbaric ideas to obligation and rectitude."—*Dundee Advertiser.*

"The subjects chosen are extremely interesting, and contain a quantity of out-of-the-way and not easily accessible information. . . . Very tastefully printed and bound."—*Birmingham Daily Gazette.*

"The book is handsomely got up; the style throughout is popular and clear, and the variety of its contents, and the individuality of the writers gave an added charm to the work."—*Daily Free Press.*

"The book is interesting both to the general reader and the student."—*Cheshire Notes and Queries.*

"Those who care only to be amused will find plenty of entertainment in this volume, while those who regard it as a work of reference will rejoice at the variety of material, and appreciate the careful indexing."—*Dundee Courier.*

"Very interesting subjects, lucidly and charmingly written. The versatility of the work assures for it a wide popularity."—*Northern Gazette.*

"A happy and useful addition to current literature."—*Norfolk Chronicle.*

"The book is a very fascinating one, and it is specially interesting to students of history as showing the vast changes which, by gradual course of development have been brought about both in the principles and practice of the law."—*The Evening Gazette.*

Bygone Southwark.

BY MRS. E. BOGER.

Demy 8vo., Cloth gilt, 7s. 6d. Numerous Illustrations.

CONTENTS:—Historical Southwark and London Bridge—Ecclesiastical Southwark—Literary and Dramatic Southwark—Local and Antiquarian Southwark—The Industries of Southwark—Amusements of Southwark—Odds and Ends, Shreds and Patches—Index.

"An attractive volume."—*The Standard.*

"A popular and interesting volume. . . . . It will be prized by the local historian and antiquary, and will be read with delight by all interested in London annals. Its illustrations include views of St. Saviour's Church and reproductions of the Frost Fair, the Globe Theatre, the interior of the Swan Theatre by De Witt, the old Tabard Inn, old London Bridge, and other spots of high interest."—*Notes and Queries.*

Bygone Berkshire.

EDITED BY THE REV. P. H. DITCHFIELD, M.A., F.S.A.

Demy 8vo., Cloth gilt, 7s. 6d. Numerous Illustrations.

CONTENTS:—Historic Berkshire—Windsor Castle—Wallingford Castle—Cumnor Place and Amy Robsart—Alfred the Great—The Guilds of Berkshire—The Scouring of the White Horse—The Last of the Abbots—Siege of Reading—Reading Abbey—The First Battle of Newbury—The Second Battle of Newbury—Binfield and Easthampstead 1700-1716, and the Early Years of Alexander Pope—Berkshire Words and Phrases—Bull-Baiting in Berkshire—Index.

"'Bygone Berkshire' is a welcome addition to a series which we have often favourably noticed."—*The Times.*

"The volume is a handsome one, and its many illustrations have been carefully drawn."—*Reading Mercury.*

Bygone Somerset.

EDITED BY CUMING WALTERS.

Demy 8vo., Cloth gilt, 7s. 6d.

CONTENTS:—Somerset County—Sedgemoor and Monmouth Rebellion—Taunton and the Bloody Assize—Cliffs and Caverns—The Lead Mines of the Mendips—The Legends and Antiquities of Glastonbury—A Note on the Cathedral City of Wells—Church Bell Inscriptions—The Christian Symbol in Wood and Stone—The Camelot of History and Romance—Roman and Fashionable Bath—Clevedon: a Literary Shrine—Superstitious and Curious Events—Cider Songs and Customs—The Lansdown Bagdad and its Caliph—The Learned Friar of Ilchester—Queen Elizabeth's Godson—The Inland Sanctuaries—"Quorum Reliquæ Hic Sunt—The City and County of Bristol—Index.

"There is much that is readable and very enjoyable in its pages . . . The illustrations are excellent, and we can recommend this book to our readers with confidence."—*Bristol Times and Mirror.*

"Forms a most valuable addition to any library."—*Clevedon Mercury.*

Bygone Sussex.
By W. E. A. AXON.

Demy 8vo., Cloth gilt, 7s. 6d. Numerous Illustrations.

CONTENTS :—The Land of the South Saxons—Pardon Brasses—Trial of Henry Robson in 1598—In Denis Duval's Country—The Long Man of Wilmington—The True Maid of the South—'Old Humphrey's' Grave—A Mediæval Legend of Winchelsea—Poems of Sussex Places—Spirits at Brightling in 1659—The Monstrous Child of Chichester—A Ruskin Pilgrimage—Rye in the Sixteenth and Seventeenth Centuries—The Merchant of Chichester—Drayton's Song of Sussex—A Sussex Book—The Mercer's Son of Midhurst—The Drummer of Herstmonceux—Sussex Sun-Dials—Tunbridge Wells Early in the Eighteenth Century—The Miller's Tomb—The Sussex Muse—Index.

"It is a most acceptable addition to Sussex literature."—*Brighton Herald.*

"A handsome volume."—*Manchester Guardian.*

"A very pleasant miscellany of topics relating to the Sussex of the past."—*The Times.*

Bygone Scotland.
By DAVID MAXWELL, C.E.

Demy 8vo., Cloth gilt, 7s. 6d. Numerous Illustrations.

CONTENTS :—The Roman Conquest of Britain—Britain as a Roman Province—The Anglo-Saxons in Britain—The Rise of the Scottish Nation—The Danish Invasions of Britain—The last Two Saxon Kings of England—How Scotland became a Free Nation—Scotland in the Two Hundred Years after Bannockburn—The Older Scottish Literature—The Reformation in England and Scotland—The Rival Queens, Mary and Elizabeth—Old Edinburgh—Offences and their Punishment in the Sixteenth Century—Old Aberdeen—Witchcraft in Scotland—Holy-Wells in Scotland—Scottish Marriage Customs—Scotland under Charles the First—Scotland under Cromwell—Scotland under Charles the Second—Scotland under James the Second—The Revolution of 1688—The Massacre of Glencoe—The Union of Scotland and England—The Jacobite Risings of 1715—The Rebellion of 1745—Index.

"The book forms a splendid addition to the works of the same series all printed at the 'Hull Press,' and, like all its predecessors, is printed in the exceptionally beautiful style which marks the productions of Mr. Andrews' establishment. The volume is handsomely bound, and well illustrated Mr. Andrews is a bookmaker *par excellence*."—*Printing World.*

"Scotland is decidedly a country 'with a past,' and that past Mr. Maxwell has here made real to us in a handsome volume, which is at once entertaining and instructive. All interested in the history of North Britain may be confidently recommended to add Mr. Maxwell's work to their shelves."—*Publishers' Circular.*

"A worthy addition to a series which has more than once been mentioned and commended in this place."—*The Times.*

Bygone Cheshire.

Edited by WILLIAM ANDREWS, f.r.h.s.

Demy 8vo., Cloth gilt, 7s. 6d.   Numerous Illustrations.

Contents :—Historic Cheshire—King Edgar on the Dee—Chester Castle and Walls—Chester Cathedral—Festival Time in Old Chester—Chester Fair—The Origin of the Rows of Chester—Old Chester Houses—The Dee Mills and " The Miller of the Dee "—Hugh Lupus—The Plague in Cheshire—Ancient Eddisbury—St. Peter's Chains : an Old Congleton Custom—Was Mary Fitton Shakespeare's " Dark Lady " ?—Sandbach Over Sixty Years Ago—Ancient Bridges, Fords, and Ferries—Cheshire Proverbial Phrases—A Souling Song—President Bradshaw—Thomas Parnell, Poet—Bishop Heber—Punishing Scolding Women—Index.

" Mr. William Andrews has produced a very attractive and interesting volume."—*Liverpool Post.*

" A high standard of literary merit is preserved throughout."—*Chester Courant.*

" The twenty-odd chapters which comprise this handsome volume are for the most part the productions of different authors, every one of whom has made a special study of the subject upon which he writes.   As a result of this happy arrangement, a varied and entertaining, as well as a reliable and instructive, treatise of ' Bygone Cheshire' is presented."—*Liverpool Mercury.*

Bygone Nottinghamshire.

By WILLIAM STEVENSON.

Demy 8vo., Cloth gilt, 7s. 6d.   Numerous Illustrations.

Contents :—The Wapentakes—The Origin of the County—The Origin of the Town—The Earliest Recorded Visitors to the County—The Suppression of the Knights Templars—Old Sanctuary Days—Notable Instances of Sanctuary—A Note on the Beverley Sanctuary—The King's Gallows of the County—The Reign of Terror in Notts.—Public Executions—Old Family Feuds—Visitations of the Plague—Visitation in the Town—Visitations in the County—Nottingham Goose Fair—The Great Priory Fair at Lenton—The Pilgrimage of Grace—The Pilgrim Fathers ; or the Founders of New England—The Descendants of the Pilgrim Fathers—Archieopiscopal Palaces—The Ancient Inns and Taverns of Nottingham—Index.

" Mr. William Stevenson's book is a useful addition to the literature of the county, and in doing so we cheerfully offer a word of praise to the printer and publisher.   Mr. William Andrews has done his part of the work admirably, and, seeing that he is a Notts. man, and himself an able and industrious antiquary, it must have been to him ' a labour of love.'"—*Newark Advertiser.*

" A most pleasant addition to local history."—*Nottingham Daily Guardian.*

The Story of Mollie.

By MARIAN BOWER,
Author of "Paynton Jacks Gentleman," etc.
Crown 8vo.   Price 3s. 6d.

"A rather unusual child is the subject of this pretty story. Troubled with a highly-sensitive brain, and exceedingly self-contained, the poor child's actions are generally misunderstood until a grown-up cousin appears on the scene, and a bond of sympathy is established. The young man seems instinctively to read the child's character, and thenceforward happiness is the lot of the despised little Mollie. Not for long, however. A catastrophe happens, and the quaint child-mind undergoes a terrible struggle, out of which she issues scathless. There are other characters in the story, all of whom play their parts well. A perusal of the book leaves in the mind a picture of a little child's soul struggling upwards through darkness and worldly surroundings. The book is well written, and, as is usual with this firm, beautifully produced.—*Liverpool Mercury.*

"The volume is one on which the author may be congratulated. It is full of charm, and, though written with studied simplicity, is clever beyond the ordinary, and obviously comes from one who has thought much on the mysteries and perplexities of existence."—*Birmingham Daily Gazette.*

"It is a touching picture of neglected child-life, which does not arouse the sympathy and affection of those who ought to cherish and study it. . . . The real merit of the story lies in the way in which the very delicate and unusual relationship is managed. Any failure in this would have ruined the story, which is, as it reads, unaffectedly strong and well written."—*Leeds Mercury.*

"No one can fail to enjoy the sweetness of 'The Story of Mollie,' nor to appreciate the delicate and subtle grace with which the author has told it. It does one good to find among so many worthless stories of to-day one that embodies so much sweetness and truth as well as strength."—*Boston Times.*

Old Grimsby.

By the REV. GEORGE SHAW.
Demy 8vo, cloth gilt, 7s. 6d.   Numerous illustrations.

CONTENTS:—The Old Town—British and Roman Times—The Anglo-Saxon Period—The Danish Period—Grimsby after the Conquest—The Old Borough—The Old Church—Early Trade and Commerce—Sports and Pastimes—Grimsby Families and Notabilities—Members of Parliament—Mayors—Condition of the People—The Marshes—Elections—Religious and other Institutions—Educational—Bibliography—Index.

"Mr. Shaw's volume is one of the greatest interest to all in any way connected with Grimsby and at all desirous of knowing something about the town, and its government in the old old days, a picturesque period and a time alive with that kind of reminiscence always so acceptable when old things have passed away and all things become new."—*Grimsby News.*

"Not only to the reader who is specially concerned with Grimsby, but also to the historical student, the book comes as a boon. Clearness of diction, breadth of view, and authentic siftings from the best authorities, render the work an important contribution to the history of England itself."—*The Eastern Daily Telegraph.*

"An interesting book."—*Eastern Morning News.*

Essex in the Days of Old.

EDITED BY JOHN T. PAGE.

Demy 8vo, cloth gilt, 7s. 6d.   Numerous illustrations.

CONTENTS :—Witchcraft in Essex—Charles Dickens and Chigwell—Hadleigh Castle—Daniel Defoe in Essex—Harbottle Grimston, Puritan and Patriot—In the Reign of Terror—John Locke and Oates—The Homes and Haunts of Elizabeth Fry—The Notorious Dean of Bocking and the "Eikon Basilike"—Barking Abbey—The Round Church of Little Maplestead—Waltham Holy Cross—Queen Elizabeth in Essex—The Salmons and Haddocks of Leigh—The Dutch Refugees and the Bay and Say Trade—John Strype and Leyton—The Brass of Archbishop Harsnett—Old Southend—The Bartlow Hills—Index.

" An extremely interesting and useful contribution to historic literature."
—*East Anglian Times.*

" An attractive volume."—*Norfolk Chronicle.*

" The volume is choicely illustrated, and should attract readers far beyond the county of which it treats."—*Birmingham Daily Gazette.*

" It is a readable and useful book."—*The Times.*

Yorkshire Family Romance.

BY FREDERICK ROSS, F.R.H.S.

Elegantly bound in cloth gilt, Demy 8vo., 6s.

CONTENTS :—The Synod of Streoneshalh—The Doomed Heir of Osmotherley—St. Eadwine, the Royal Martyr—The Viceroy Siward—Phases in the Life of a Political Martyr—The Murderer's Bride—The Earldom of Wiltes—Blackfaced Clifford—The Shepherd Lord—The Felons of Ilkley—The Ingilby Boar's Head—The Eland Tragedy—The Plumpton Marriage—The Topcliffe Insurrection—Burning of Cottingham Castle—The Alum Workers—The Maiden of Marblehead—Rise of the House of Phipps—The Traitor Governor of Hull.

" The grasp and thoroughness of the writer is evident in every page, and the book forms a valuable addition to the literature of the North Country."
The Gentlewoman.

" Many will welcome this work."—*Yorkshire Post.*

Legendary Yorkshire.

BY FREDERICK ROSS, F.R.H.S.

Elegantly bound in cloth gilt, Demy 8vo., 6s.

CONTENTS :—The Enchanted Cave—The Doomed City—The Worm of Nunnington—The Devil's Arrows—The Giant Road Maker of Mulgrave—The Virgin's Head of Halifax—The Dead Arm of St. Oswald the King—The Translation of St. Hilda—A Miracle of St. John—The Beatified Sisters—The Dragon of Wantley—The Miracles and Ghost of Watton—The Murdered Hermit of Eskdale—The Calverley Ghost—The Bewitched House of Wakefield.

" It is a work of lasting interest, and cannot fail to delight the reader."
—*Beverley Recorder.*

" The history and the literature of our county are now receiving marked attention, and Mr. Andrews merits the support of the public for the production of this and other interesting volumes he has issued. We cannot speak too highly of this volume, the printing, the paper, and the binding being faultless."—*Driffield Observer.*

www.ingramcontent.com/pod-product-compliance
Lightning Source LLC
Chambersburg PA
CBHW030409170426
43202CB00010B/1543